SUPERDOCIOUS!

SUPERDOCIOUS!

RACING INSIGHTS AND REVELATIONS
FROM LEGENDARY OLYMPIC SAILOR
RODNEY PATTISSON

RODNEY PATTISSON

WITH BARRY PICKTHALL

ADLARD COLES

LONDON • OXFORD • NEW YORK • NEW DELHI • SYDNEY

ADLARD COLES
Bloomsbury Publishing Plc
50 Bedford Square, London, WC1B 3DP, UK

BLOOMSBURY, ADLARD COLES and the Adlard Coles logo are
trademarks of Bloomsbury Publishing Plc

First published in Great Britain 2019

A catalogue record for this book is available from the British Library

Library of Congress Cataloguing-in-Publication data has been applied for

ISBN: HB: 978-1-4729-3559-5; eBook: 978-1-4729-3560-1

2 4 6 8 10 9 7 5 3 1

Typeset in Haarlemmer MT Std by Deanta Global Publishing Services,
Chennai, India
Printed and bound in Great Britain by CPI Group (UK) Ltd, Croydon CR0 4YY

To find out more about our authors and books visit www.bloomsbury.com
and sign up for our newsletters

CONTENTS

FOREWORD

From a very early age, sailing Optimist dinghies, Rodney Pattisson was my boyhood hero: someone whom I and many others from my generation looked up to and tried to emulate. To us, he was our hero figure.

I had read that Rodney and that other great Olympic sailor, Denmark's Paul Elvstrøm, were the first to pioneer a dedicated approach to sailing, by living and breathing the sport and developing a comprehensive understanding of the science and design that make boats go fast, and I worked hard to follow this.

I first met Rodney in 2003 while racing during Cowes Week. I was 26, and though by that stage I had managed to win Olympic gold and silver medals, I was still very much in awe of his reputation. It is often said that when you finally meet your childhood hero, you invariably come away disillusioned, but this was not at all the case. To my delight, I found him both modest and understated but with a certain aura about him.

My job on board was to steer the boat, but I felt duty-bound to offer him the wheel. He declined and soon put me at ease. 'No, this is your gig. I'm very happy to be in the background,' he replied. We got on really well. He gave me the right input about wind, bearings and the whereabouts of other boats, and even though the race was relatively low-key you could sense an underlying competitive streak. It was a great introduction and happily we have remained in touch ever since.

I hope that Rodney's inspiring life story, told here for the first time, will spur future generations of young sailors to match, and even exceed, the successes achieved by British Olympians to date.

Sir Ben Ainslie CBE
Four-time Olympic medal winner and America's Cup skipper who was inspired by Rodney Pattisson's Olympic successes to take up sail racing himself

Sir Ben Ainslie CBE and Rodney Pattison MBE at the opening of Parkstone Yacht Club in Poole, Dorset in August 2018. © Jane Southern.

What marks out a champion?

Admiral Michael Cecil Boyce, Baron Boyce KG, GCB, OBE, DL, the former First Sea Lord and Chief of the Defence Staff who graduated from Dartmouth Naval College with Rodney Pattisson, and crewed for him in his first Flying Dutchman campaign.

We all have our strong points and contrasting character traits. With some, the curve is relatively fair, but others have a huge spike within their psychometric make-up, a brilliant streak balanced by other traits that fall below the norm.

Rodney Pattisson is one of the latter. He's a very bright guy and a total perfectionist. Nothing sways his attention away from winning and he drives himself just as hard as he does his crew. No stone is left unturned – from levels of fitness to the minutiae of stranding down cotton telltales to signal the slightest zephyr, sanding down a surface to micrometre levels or applying serious mathematics and mechanics to make a fast boat go even faster. He does it all with a level of focus and blinkered dedication that few would even wish to aspire to. These are the traits that mark him out as a champion.

We first met in September 1961 when joining the Royal Navy as officer cadets at Dartmouth Naval College. At the time, I was not a sailor in any sense and we moved in different circles. My interests centred on rugby and squash, and sailing was not on my agenda, other than to know enough to gain my qualifications.

Rodney came to my attention when we were learning to sail the heavy and ungainly naval cutters on the River Dart. He had already won the Cadet Class national championship, and everyone

1

tried to copy whatever he did. Most of us didn't have much idea, so when Rodney pulled on a rope, we did the same, and attempted to follow his approach to the start line – at which point Rodney simply shot ahead.

Even then we didn't really realise how good a sailor he was. At Dartmouth, we spent the first term simply adjusting to naval life. For the second term, the year intake is split, with one half going to sea while the rest stay behind to study. We remained scattered across the fleet during our second year, too, so it was not until our third year that I got to know Rodney for the first time. It was September 1963 and we found ourselves within a class of eight selected for our abilities in maths and science. Rodney has a really scientific mind and spent most of this time applying what we learned from advanced physics and hydrodynamics to calculate how to make a boat sail faster.

Rodney approached me at the beginning of 1964 to see if I would be interested in joining him racing a Flying Dutchman. I had not heard of the class before and my sailing experience was no less vague. The reasons I think he picked me over others with far greater experience were, first, because I wouldn't argue or present any sort of problem; and second, I was 6ft 2.32in (1.89m) tall, weighed exactly 12 stone 5.37lb (78.64kg) and was extremely fit. I met his criteria for the perfect FD crew exactly, which underlines the perfectionism he brings to every level. Whenever we went sailing, for instance, he would review the conditions and tell me exactly what to wear – a particular dry jumper, plus two wet jumpers on top perhaps – so that my weight was correct to the nearest ounce for the wind conditions he expected on the day.

This perfectionism extended to the cotton telltales on the shrouds. How much do they weigh? Very little, but he would strand down the cotton to the very minimum to indicate the slightest puff of wind. His attention to specifics was always incredible and he would spend hours sanding down the hull or foils, rubbing away a few microns here or there to get a perfect fairness of line.

I could live with this very easily because I was on a vertical learning curve. I simply did as I was told and learned a huge amount. It's likely, however, that anyone else with greater knowledge than

I had would have been driven insane by this fastidious attention to detail and would not have been able to work with him.

During our training prior to the Olympic trials in 1964 I stayed at Rodney's family home in Poole and found everyone showed this same attention to detail. Living in that environment for ten days was an extraordinary experience. It was total immersion and it gave me a joy for sailing that I have carried with me ever since.

Although we didn't win those Olympic trials in 1964, Rodney put in a really respectable performance in a class of boat that we had only started sailing a few months before. This, I realised later, was the start of his single-minded preparations for an assault on the world championships and the Olympic Games in 1968.

Others have undoubtedly found Rodney difficult to understand, but he and I got on well together, mainly because I didn't have the knowledge to argue and I was keen to learn. I would have liked to have continued to crew for him on his route to Olympic stardom because I found both Rodney and the sport so fascinating. However, after the trials and graduation from Dartmouth as sub-lieutenants, our worlds began to divide. I wanted to pursue a career in the Navy, while Rodney made it quite clear that sailboat racing was his number one priority.

He stayed in submarines for a while, and the tolerance level within his wardroom must have been pretty high, for while it was great to work with a world-class sailor and potential Olympic champion, his fellow officers had to pick up Rodney's duties during his frequent disappearances, which put quite a strain on the command.

Rodney is one of those people military men describe as 'brilliant in war ... bloody awful in peacetime'. The latter might be exaggerated here, but he is not political by nature and compromise is not within his vocabulary. In any war situation, his ruthless single-minded approach – the very same qualities that have made him such a successful competitor – would have been invaluable.

Having met his father, a World War II flying ace, I sense that Rodney inherited many of his strong traits from this side of his family, for Lieutenant-Commander Ken Pattisson displayed exactly the same ruthless execution that I would expect from Rodney when he fired the torpedo from his Swordfish biplane with such precision that it is likely that it disabled the German battleship *Bismarck* during World War II.

It doesn't surprise me to learn that Rodney has total recall of every tack, gybe and mark rounding in just about every race. There are top golfers who can tell you the same many years later about their third tee shot on to the ninth green at a particular course. This is how champions make sure that they learn from every incident and correct themselves next time around. It is this formidable attention to detail that sets champions and gold medallists apart.

In peacetime, though, you can't expect to win every battle, and have to use more devious means, which is not something that suits Rodney's temperament. This is shown in his 30-year battle to reverse Prime Minister Edward Heath's decision not to award Chris Davies an MBE after the two won gold at the 1972 Olympic Games in Kiel, and from his run-in with senior sporting officials, which led to Rodney being barred from running with the Olympic torch prior to the 2012 Games. Yet, just as significantly, it was his extreme persistence that eventually won the day in both cases.

Without these extreme traits, Rodney Pattisson would perhaps never have become one of Britain's most successful sailors, winning three Olympic medals and 18 dinghy and offshore championships.

It is quite a record.

ONE

Early years

I was born in Campbeltown, Argyll on 5 August 1943 while my father, Kenneth Pattisson, a pilot in the Fleet Air Arm, was posted there for a short period as the air gunnery training instructor for the torpedo-carrying Fairey Swordfish biplanes capable of attacking German warships and detecting U-boats.

I was the second eldest of four siblings and lived there with my elder sister Penny for just a few months. We then moved south, living in a bungalow in Gurnard on the Isle of Wight, owned by my grandfather, while my father was serving on aircraft carriers in the Far East. Our view out over the Solent was close to where my father had been brought up, and sailing was a major part of family life.

Both my parents were English and I've always identified myself with the same red-and-white hue, but Pattisson, being a Scottish surname, has encouraged those looking for Celtic heroes to try and paint me in blue and white. In 2002, I unwittingly allowed my name to be inducted into the newly formed Scottish Sports Hall of Fame to join a 50-strong list of sporting greats, including Olympic runner Eric Liddell; footballers Billy Bremner, Matt Busby, Bill Shankly, Kenny Dalglish, Dennis Law and Ally McCoist; motor racing champions Jim Clark, Jackie Stewart and Colin McRae; and sailing pioneer Chay Blyth.

When somebody from the Hall of Fame first rang me, I simply didn't realise the consequences. I told them I wasn't Scottish but they convinced me that it didn't matter. They said being born in Campbeltown was good enough. The fact that I had not been back to Scotland since then didn't appear to matter. I gathered they were short of Olympic gold medallists and wanted to bill my 1968 success as the first by a Scot since Dundee boxer Dick McTaggart won gold in 1956.

The impact only became apparent with the growth of the World Wide Web a decade later. I'm not anti-Scottish, but when Google and Wikipedia were telling the world I am a Scot, it all became rather embarrassing. Most people would not like to be labelled with the wrong nationality and to have to read it again and again. I wanted the facts to be correct and the only way was to ask to be removed as an inductee.

My grandfather, John, owned an exhibition company that in 1922 organised the first London Boat Show at the Agricultural Halls, Islington, which King George V, another keen sailor, visited. My grandfather owned several cruising yachts over the years, and it was probably in one of these fine vessels that I went sailing for the first time as a baby, strapped into the cockpit.

My father's role in the sinking of the *Bismarck*

It was undoubtedly a combination of seamanship and flying skills that led to my father being credited as the most likely pilot to have crippled the 50,000-ton German battleship *Bismarck* on 26 May 1941. The attack by Fairey Swordfish biplane torpedo bombers launched from the British aircraft carrier HMS *Ark Royal* led to two direct hits on the German flagship, one of which was from Pattisson's 'String bag', as these slow World War II vintage canvas-clad biplanes were called. The blast jammed the starboard rudder of the German flagship against the central propeller and left her turning in circles and at the mercy of the British fleet. It was his seamanship that led to the hit, for as he swooped down to start his bombing run, he noticed the *Bismarck* starting to turn and adjusted his sights to compensate for her anticipated change of course – something only a sailor would have been able to allow for at the very last minute.

Just two days previously the *Bismarck* had sunk, with her first salvo, HMS *Hood* – the pride of the Royal Navy – during the Battle of the Denmark Strait. The loss of life had been devastating, with all but three of *Hood*'s hands perishing, and the British Home Fleet was consequently ordered by Winston Churchill to avenge her loss at the earliest opportunity.

The German fleet had managed to give the slip to their British pursuers, and only after an intense air/sea search had a lone Catalina flying boat finally spotted *Bismarck* steaming in an easterly direction about 700 miles (1,125km) out from the French port of Brest at 10.30 on 26 May.

A Fairey Swordfish piloted by 'Tan' Tivy, who later became my godfather, took off from *Ark Royal* with a specially fitted long-range fuel tank sitting in the observer's cockpit, in order to relieve the Catalina aircraft and continue the shadowing of the *Bismarck*, circling just out of range of her guns, and so monitor the battleship's position for the next five long hours. As an experienced pilot, and realising he was running short of fuel in his main tank, Tivy switched to the long-range tank, only to have the Pegasus engine fail. Switching back to his main and emergency reserve tank, to his relief the engine fired again, but he had no option but to curtail his shadowing and head back to *Ark Royal* as fast as he could. As he came in to land the engine started spluttering badly from fuel starvation. He was on his last drop and the weather was so bad that the carrier's deck was heaving up and down some 60ft (18m). Tivy's plane missed all the arrestor wires and he was saved only by the tailhook snagging the top of the steel crash barrier protecting other aircraft parked on the flight deck. It was a lucky escape, for had his plane crashed into them, the damage would have undoubtedly prevented any further attacks on the German battleship. Instead, he walked away with just a bent propeller, a problem he reported to his mechanic. He was later told by the mechanic that the problem had indeed been fuel starvation; no one had got around to filling the long-range fuel tank!

In atrocious conditions, Sub-Lieutenant Pattisson was at the controls of one of fourteen Swordfish which took off from *Ark Royal's* spray-swept flight deck later that day to attack their prey. What the naval airmen had not been warned about was that HMS *Sheffield* had also been despatched to shadow the *Bismarck*, and as they approached in poor visibility, the contact they were obtaining on their radar screens was the shadowing British cruiser, not the German battleship.

Most of the aircraft crews went ahead and released their torpedoes. Only three pilots, including Pattisson, recognised the

Town Class cruiser in time to hold their fire. Mercifully, faults in the magnetic firing devices led to most of the torpedoes exploding on impact with the water rather than against the ship's side, and skilful handling of his ship on the part of *Sheffield*'s captain enabled her to evade the rest.

The 810 Squadron flight crews returned to *Ark Royal* totally unaware that they had attacked a British warship, and angry about the failure of their weapons. However, the lesson had been learned – the proximity heads were unreliable – and so for their next sortie the magnetic triggers were replaced with contact pistols. The torpedoes were also set to run at a shallower depth – a reconfiguration that was to prove decisive.

At 19.10, 15 Fairey Swordfish from 810, 818 and 820 Squadrons commanded by Lieutenant-Commander TP Coode took off from *Ark Royal* in very poor visibility and low cloud. My father was one of a flight of three consigned to attack the *Bismarck* independently from the starboard side. Two of them, Pattisson and Godfrey-Faussett (the third had lost contact), dived down through thick cloud to attack. Trying to launch their single torpedo at 900 yards (823m) from an altitude of 90ft (27m) at a speed of 90 knots, they dropped their fish and turned, zigzagging away to evade the German anti-aircraft fire and even the huge 15in shells being aimed their way.

To complicate matters, the pilot had to calculate the angle of 'aim off' to take account of the ship's estimated speed, and to set the torpedo off on the right collision course ahead of her bow. To achieve this, the Swordfish was equipped with a line of lights set along the upper wing ahead of the pilot. Each light was spaced along the wing at 5-knot increments up to 35 knots.

What my father spotted in the fading light as he dived down towards his target was *Bismarck* heeling to starboard. This was because seconds before, Lindemann, *Bismarck*'s captain, had started to turn his ship hard to port to present the smallest target possible against the torpedoes dropped at her port side from the first attack of five aircraft. It was Pattisson's seamanlike eye that made the difference. In the split second before firing, he made an allowance for the alteration of course, changing the aiming light before releasing his torpedo. Miraculously, his torpedo hit

Bismarck's unprotected, unarmoured aft steering compartment and the explosion jammed her twin rudders hard to port, buckling the starboard one firmly against the ship's central propeller.

Both navigators reported 'torpedoes running true' but couldn't verify hits, since neither could possibly hang around to look if they wanted to survive. The other hit on *Bismarck*'s port side was launched by Tony Beale. Having lost contact with my dad's flight, he returned to HMS *Sheffield* and got a new bearing by lamp for *Bismarck* once more, this time alone. Amazingly, the Germans thought the attack had finished and only fired at him as he fled away. His torpedo hit amidships, causing no damage due to the 12in heavy armoured plating that protected the ship from any torpedo damage. Like my father, he was honoured with a DSC for bravery.

Later, my father, always modest, told me that it was quite likely that it was his torpedo that had hit, but others in his squadron who had seen the large column of water rise up on her starboard side right aft were more certain. Sub-Lieutenant PB Meadway, my father's observer at the time, was also more positive, writing in his log: 'Attack successful, 1 probable hit.'

Crippled by the explosion, *Bismarck* spent the rest of the night steering round in circles as her crew worked desperately to free the rudders within the flooded compartment. It was to no avail. At first light the following morning, HMS *King George V* and HMS *Rodney* pounded the battleship. My father and his flight watched from the air as *Bismarck* capsized, leaving the heads of survivors 'bobbing like turnips in a field'.

In September 1941, my father left HMS *Ark Royal* in Gibraltar to return to the UK to retrain as an Air Gunnery Training Officer, and embarked on the Pegasus-Class fighter catapult ship HMS *Springbank* escorting Convoy HG 73 bound for Liverpool. All went well until a German Focke-Wulf FW 200 Condor patrol plane off Cape St Vincent spotted the 25-ship flotilla. It was chased away by a Fairey Fulmar fighter plane launched from HMS *Springbank*, but not before reporting the convoy's position, which was relayed to Italian submarines lying in wait west of Gibraltar and the German U-boats based in Bordeaux. The German U-boats sighted the convoy on the night of 26/27 September and attacked three ships. HMS *Springbank* was hit by a torpedo fired from *U-201*, which led to a race against time to evacuate her 233 crew. Three Royal Navy ships, HMS *Hibiscus*, HMS *Jasmine* and HMS *Periwinkle*, took it in turns to raft up against the stricken *Springbank* in heavy seas to give her crew the chance to jump ship. It was very much a leap of faith. Some misjudged the gap and fell to their deaths between the ships, but many more, including my father, were injured but at least survived, jumping from a considerable height in darkness on to the destroyer's heaving deck.

The start of my love affair with sailing

In 1952, my father returned from Korea, where he had served on the carrier HMS *Theseus*, and the family moved to Swanage, where he and I built a *Yachting World* Cadet dinghy from a kit of parts. DIY was never one of his strong suits and I well remember the trouble we had first steaming and then fastening the wooden keel down on to the frame. The Cadet has quite a bit of rocker at the forward end and each time we tried to bend the wood down and screw it to the boat's stubby transom it would try to spring back up, lifting the front end of the frame off the floor. We got it right in the end, and the boat measured with the minimum amount of rocker permitted under the rules – a shape, we had no idea at the time, that would make *Swallow* such a fast boat.

During the summer months, Swanage Sailing Club became a second home to us Pattisson children. By all accounts I was quite competitive. My elder sister Penny jumped overboard and swam ashore after I shouted at her, and on another day I somehow broke the tiller extension over brother John's head. I don't recall being so precocious, but this perhaps was an early sign of my need for perfection.

My father retired from the Royal Navy in 1956 and took over the reins of the family exhibition business. He was now at home for much of the time and took me, with John as crew, to compete in our first Cadet open meeting at Torquay. We won, and I remember thinking that I might be good at this sailing game.

At the age of 11, I was sent off to board at Pangbourne Naval College, as it was known then, in Berkshire and was allowed to take the Cadet with me to race on the River Thames. I loved it, and before long became captain of the college sailing team, which remained unbeaten in inter-school championships throughout my two years' tenure. I was sailing at every opportunity and absorbing new knowledge all the time, learning how to get the best from my boat in the fickle shifting winds that any tree-lined river provides.

In the six decades that have passed since, I find it quite amazing how sailing has advanced. These days, windsurfers and kiteboarders blast along at an easy 25 knots, International Moths become foil-borne in only 8 knots of wind and clock similar speeds, and the Atlantic sailing record is now lower than the best Blue Ribbon time set by the great liners crossing from New York to the Lizard.

The first synthetic sails were produced in the late 1950s. Before that, cotton was the norm, and sails had to be handled with extreme care to retain their shape. Cotton suffered from shrinkage and had to be broken in gently, rather like a new car engine in those days. This involved gently stretching the cotton threads in light winds, and only when fully stretched in were they used for racing. Just as tiresome, all the salt had to be carefully hosed off after every outing before they were hung up to dry. All ropes were cotton, too, and the Cadet even had cotton lanyards to secure the shrouds to the chain plate fittings. These were tensioned up prior to a race, but back on shore they needed to be eased off to allow for shrinkage in the rain. Failing to do this inevitably resulted in the lanyards eventually breaking and the mast falling down in the dinghy park.

Back then, Cadets were generally home-built and, like *Swallow*, constructed from a kit of parts. When completed, we proudly took *Swallow* down to our local sailing club at Swanage, where wise old sailors peered down at her with a mixture of incredulity and disdain. They thought that only clinker-built Royal Naval Sailing Association or Island Class 14ft (4.25m) dinghies were suitable for sailing in the bay, especially when an easterly onshore wind was blowing. They are solid boats, so heavy that they had to be slid up and down the shingle beach on wooden rollers. By contrast, our 10ft 6in (3.2m) plywood-constructed Cadet with its unseaworthy transom-shaped bow was so light that it could easily be lifted up and down the beach. Dinghy sailing was certainly on the change!

The Cadet was affordable and at that time clubs were adopting the class, forming squadrons up and down the country;

we eventually had more than 40 at Swanage Sailing Club. It is an ideal junior training boat, too uncomfortable for adults to sail, and it gave me a first opportunity to win races locally against other children. Within a couple of years we had the biggest class and most competitive racing the club had ever seen. The reason for its success was the brilliant vision of her designer, Jack Holt, who had drawn a dinghy suitable only for children. Sailed two up, she has a spinnaker, which in many respects made her a better junior trainer than the Optimist single-hander. Cadets often stay in the family for many years; I still have mine after all the Pattisson children learned to sail in her, the younger ones starting out crewing for their older siblings.

There were a few open meetings to go to, such as my first at Torquay, but Cadet Week at Burnham-on-Crouch was always the main event, sailed under the auspices of the Royal Corinthian YC, which had dormitories to accommodate us all. *Yachting World* magazine adopted the boat from the outset, carrying a Cadet section in every edition, and Group Captain Haylock, its editor, always took a keen interest in this annual championship.

My first Nationals took place in 1959. Still with my 'cottons', I found myself competing against the best Cadet sailors around, all using new Terylene sails – an unequal situation that I had no understanding of at the time, but one that, as it turned out, became a blessing in disguise the following year.

The event always attracted strong foreign entries, including a group from Belgium who took it very seriously. Indeed, they even had a team manager, which was something unheard of in those days. Interestingly, the winner in 1959 was Jacques Rogge, who went on to win the Finn-Class World Championship, and who represented Belgium at three Olympic Games and ended his career as president of the International Olympic Committee.

I returned to Burnham the following year with brother John crewing and armed with a new set of synthetic sails, anxious to see what difference they would make. The Belgians, manager again in tow, were determined once more to win the regatta by all possible means. Comparing overall results from the previous year when I had finished tenth – the top boat with 'cottons' – they asterisked the serious opposition and compiled their hit list. Luckily for me,

I didn't feature, since they failed to appreciate my handicapped performance.

With new sails, *Swallow* was transformed, and we won some of the early races. Burnham-on-Crouch is not the easiest of places for racing. Winds invariably blow up and down the river, and when sailing against the tide you have to short tack close to the bank to lessen its effect. The Cadet's vertical daggerboard was of no help here. The nearer the bank, the more you gained, until of course the board got stuck in the mud and became very difficult to lift, however hard the crew tugged at it.

Group Captain Haylock took it upon himself that year to display the event standings on the eve of the final race. To the dismay of the Belgian manager, one boat, *Swallow,* crewed by John and myself, was leading, and something clearly needed to be done about it!

I still remember that last race, being sat on quite deliberately by the Belgian helmsman delegated to take us out. He looked back at me, grinning like a Cheshire cat as he covered us short tacking up the shore. There was no obvious means of escape, and by concentrating on blanketing our wind, he ensured that we both sank down the fleet. I did succeed in getting past at one point, by playing him off against another competitor and a moored boat, but then hit the mud and became a victim once more. All I could do was hang on and hope to finish with enough points. As we neared the club finish line, I took a big risk by tacking inside the piles on which the clubhouse stands, which gained me the one place I needed.

And so I won my first championship by the skin of my teeth – by a mere one-quarter point – and gained valuable lessons that stood me in good stead during my Olympic days.

Moving on to Firefly

I graduated from the Cadet to race a Firefly, which had been designed by Uffa Fox and was launched immediately after World War II by Fairey Marine as a strict one-design budget dinghy. Seven decades on, the class remains as popular as ever, with the original hot-moulded wooden hulls still competing on equal terms with the latest glass-fibre models. *Ismene* No 27 was a Mk 1 version that I purchased from Bradfield College for £25. She was one of the oldest in the fleet, still with her original aluminium decks and buoyancy tanks, and I bought a kit of plywood parts to upgrade the boat to a Mk 2 version. The kit also included a transom, which strangely had a different profile to that of the original, and fearing this might change the shape of the hull and affect the boat's performance, I never changed this. I'm glad I didn't because *Ismene* proved to be one of the fastest in the fleet, carrying me to win the Public Schools Firefly championships in 1960 and 1961.

Today, there is a gulf between even good club sailors and the professional elite who now dominate the international scene. Racing at the top level has become a full-time, very rewarding occupation. Thanks to sponsorship and government sports grants, top sailors now have their own coaches, fitness instructors, physiotherapists, dieticians and even psychologists – the same kind of support that was once only afforded to top athletes and tennis stars.

Back in the 1960s, we paid all our own expenses, camped at regattas and had to have either very supportive bosses, as I had, or a private income to cover the time away. Rivals – and some of my crews – complained that I was probably the most professional amateur within the Olympic circus, but there was another – Denmark's Paul Elvstrøm. He became the first to win four gold medals at consecutive Games, a record that stood for 52 years until it was matched by Ben Ainslie in 2012. The Dane won his first medal at the 1948 Olympic regatta in Torquay racing a Firefly, then the single-hander, before moving on to dominate the Finn Class for more than a decade. He was one of the first to understand the importance of body movement in a sailboat, took fitness to new levels, and built a bench with toe straps that mirrored the cockpit of his Finn and sat on it for hours at home to strengthen his back, torso and leg muscles. He was also very inventive, coming up with the idea for an adjustable kicking strap to control mainsail leach tension, and a venturi self-bailer, which would push back up into the hull if you grounded and had a one-way flap valve to stop water from flowing back into the boat. He also had a deep understanding of rigs, and went on to form his own sail loft and Elvstrøm mast designs, made under licence by a great friend and Flying Dutchman Class rival, Frenchman Eric Duchemin, for whom I was the British agent for a time. Elvstrøm was a perfectionist and his dedication to winning had a definite influence on my approach to sailing.

A recipe for success

Many of the factors that led to winning in my day remain just the same now:

Boat
- Down to minimum weight
- Perfect finish to bottom and foils
- The best rig and sails
- Minimum combined crew weight

Personal
- Supreme fitness and stamina
- Clean living

Preparation
- Know your boat and what makes it go fast
- Select a crew with similar ambitions
- Time in the boat: train hard so that helm and crew know instinctively what each other is doing and get boat/sail handling routines down to automatic levels
- Learn the basics about sea/land breezes and weather forecasting

Venue
- Research tidal streams and other vagaries that can affect water flow around the course
- Relate knowledge of sea/land breezes and prevailing winds to course venue and check for unique features that can deflect airflow, such as buildings, cliffs and trees
- Check high and low water times, and when tidal stream flow changes
- Note down exact course details and time of start
- Get out to start area an hour before and check wind shift and tidal patterns, set boat up for the conditions, and check for any bias on the start line

Modern developments

Although the ingredients that comprise the recipe for sailing success (see box on p.15) remain the same, there is no doubt that modern sailors have access to far more technology and professional guidance than I did. Key aspects that have changed since my dinghy days are:

Fitness
Personal fitness is now a science. Athletes have a personal trainer to develop specific circuit training in the gym, on the track and in the pool to push them to peak fitness. Physiotherapy is also key, warding off strains that would otherwise impede performance.

Sail coach
He or she will work with you to improve sailing techniques and knowledge of the environment, using video to provide detailed post-race analysis of what you and, just as importantly, your rivals did out on the race course.

Dietician
This, too, has become a science. While I made do, eating basic wholesome food served up at home and in the ship's canteen, top athletes now monitor their daily calorie count very closely and focus on eating so-called superfoods. Iain MacDonald-Smith and I did go on a strict protein-rich diet for a month prior to the 1968 Olympics in a concerted effort to each lose 1 stone (6.35kg) of weight to help our performance in the light winds of Acapulco Bay, then changed to a normal diet for the last three days before the start to build up stamina, but this was primitive dietary engineering.

There are many superfood diets, but one short-term plan that caught the attention of Sir Ben Ainslie and his BAR America's Cup crew is the sirt food diet, which not only reduces weight but also stimulates muscle growth – two important aspects when racing weight-conscious foil-borne multihulls. Sirt foods are everyday plant foods known as sirtuin activators, which switch on the 'skinny' genes usually activated by exercise and fasting. The most potent sirt foods are all readily available and include: red wine, dark chocolate, black coffee, kale, rocket, parsley, red onions, strawberries, walnuts, extra virgin olive oil, curry spices, green tea, blueberries, celery, chilli, apples and buckwheat. These can be mixed with red and white meat, fish, noodles, pasta and potatoes to provide well-balanced diets.

NB: No one should embark on an extreme diet, take fitness-enhancing supplements or any medication without medical supervision in case any ingredient has trace elements of performance-enhancing drugs. Ignorance is no defence. The athlete is held responsible for what goes into their body and if any element breaches World Anti-Doping Agency (WADA) regulations, they are labelled as cheats and banned from the sport.

Psychoanalysis

In my day psychologists were known as 'trick cyclists' and the subject was treated with utmost suspicion. Now, psychometric analysis is all part and parcel of the athlete's toolkit. This science helps you to understand your own mental strengths and weaknesses and to recognise the traits in the character make-up of your rivals, helping you to make the most of your own plus points and to exploit the negative aspects within others.

There are several psychometric tests that people can take, but one developed by Dr William Marston, a physiological psychologist who made a lifetime study of the emotions and behaviour patterns of normal people, is as accurate as any. He also invented the first functional lie-detector polygraph after discovering a correspondence between blood pressure and lying, and built a device to measure changes in a person's blood pressure while the subject was being questioned.

Dr Marston's DiSC traits

In addition to inventing the lie detector, Dr Marston came up with the theory that we are all subject to four main character traits. Some people fall into one style, others fall into two, and the profiles of others can cover three traits:

Dominance (D)
Person places emphasis on accomplishing results, the bottom line, confidence

Influence (i)
Person places emphasis on influencing or persuading others, openness, relationships

Steadiness (S)
Person places emphasis on cooperation, sincerity, dependability

Conscientiousness (C)
Person places emphasis on quality and accuracy, expertise

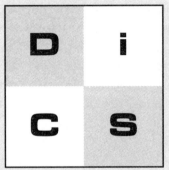

Perceives self as more powerful than the environment. Is active, fast, assertive and bold.

Perceives the environment as unfavourable. Is questioning, logic-focused, sceptical and challenging.

Perceives environment as favourable. Is accepting, people-focused, receptive and agreeable.

Perceives self as less powerful than the environment. Is thoughtful, moderate-paced, calm and careful.

My personal profile pattern

Dr Marston concluded that normal people fall into one of 15 distinct profile patterns, each with a specific blend of these DiSC traits. He did not create an instrument to measure these levels, but others have, and now it is possible to test yourself – as I did online at www.everythingdisc.co.uk. The results show that I have strong 'Developer' traits, which others who know me well say is a good summary of my characteristics:

'Emotions: Is concerned with meeting personal needs
Goal: New opportunities
Judges others by: Ability to meet my own standards

Influences others by: Pursuit of solutions for problems; projection of personal sense of power

Value to an organisation: Avoids passing the buck; seeks new or innovative problem-solving methods

Overuses: Control over people and situations to accomplish my own results

Under pressure: Works alone to complete tasks; is belligerent if individualism is threatened or challenging opportunities disappear

Fears: Boredom and loss of control

Would increase effectiveness with more: Patience, empathy; participation and collaboration with others, together with follow-through and attention to quality control.'

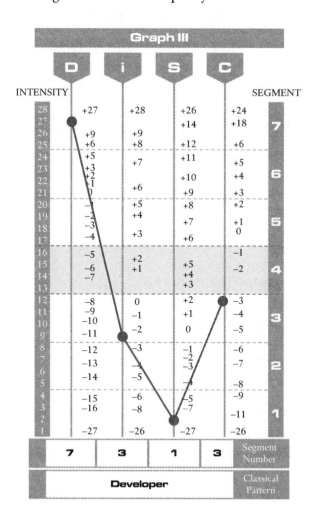

The detailed report suggests that I am high in the Dominance dimension. To achieve results, it says that I shape my environment by overcoming opposition and taking action to achieve the results, seek opportunities for advancement and individual accomplishment, and aspire to positions of power and authority. The main objectives for people like me, the report says, are control and the freedom to make quick decisions. It tells me that we are not intimidated by troubleshooting issues and solving problems, even if this means questioning the status quo. We work best when receiving difficult assignments or getting the occasional shock to our world view. We have no problem tackling a wide range of activities and tasks.

To produce our highest-quality work, we 'high Ds' need to identify with a group and to pace ourselves, which can be challenging because we dislike being controlled by others. A crew needs to work to complement these strong traits by helping to structure a predictable environment around us.

Employing caution, calculating risks and weighing the pros and cons are not our strong suits, so it may be wise for 'high Ds' to surround themselves with people who have these skills, although too often we 'high Ds' find it difficult to understand the need for this support.

Intensity index

D	i	S	C
28 egocentric	28 enthusiastic	28 passive	28 perfectionist
27 direct	27 gregarious	27 patient	27 accurate
26 daring	26 persuasive	26 loyal	26 fact-finder
25 domineering	25 impulsive	25 predictable	25 diplomatic
24 demanding	24 emotional	24 team-person	24 systematic
23 forceful	23 self-promoting	23 serene	23 conventional
22 risk-taker	22 trusting	22 possessive	22 courteous
21 adventuresome	21 influential	21 complacent	21 careful
20 decisive	20 pleasant	20 inactive	20 restrained
19 inquisitive	19 sociable	19 relaxed	19 high standards
18 self-assured	18 generous	18 nondemonstrative	18 analytical
17 competitive	17 poised	17 deliberate	17 sensitive
16 quick	16 charming	16 amiable	16 mature
15 self-reliant	15 confident	15 stable	15 evasive
14 calculated risk-taker	14 convincing	14 mobile	14 "own person"
13 self-critical	13 observing	13 outgoing	13 self-righteous
12 unassuming	12 discriminating	12 alert	12 opinionated
11 self-effacing	11 reflective	11 eager	11 persistent
10 realistic	10 factual	10 critical	10 independent
9 weighs pros and cons	9 logical	9 discontented	9 rigid
8 meek	8 controlled	8 fidgety	8 firm
7 conservative	7 retiring	7 impetuous	7 stubborn
6 peaceful	6 suspicious	6 restless	6 arbitrary
5 mild	5 pessimistic	5 change-oriented	5 rebellious
4 quiet	4 aloof	4 fault-finding	4 defiant
3 unsure	3 withdrawn	3 spontaneous	3 obstinate
2 dependent	2 self-conscious	2 frustrated by status quo	2 tactless
1 modest	1 reticent	1 active	1 sarcastic

This is what the profiling reported:
'Rodney Pattisson's DiSC score highlights the following within his D profile:

D Dimension
Egocentric: Rodney has a strong focus on meeting goals and tackling red tape, and is not distracted by heavy opposition or events.

Direct: He calls a spade, a spade. No one has to second-guess what Rodney says, but this natural bluntness can be perceived as counterproductive.

Daring: Rodney is not afraid to 'rock the boat' or take chances trying out new things.

Domineering: He is certainly goal orientated and decisive and may not always value other opinions as much as he might.

Demanding: Rodney instinctively applies pressure on others to encourage them to achieve the desired results. This is a natural strength that can work well in focusing a crew towards winning, but some fail to understand this trait and find this overbearing.

i Dimension

Discriminating: Rodney has the ability to discriminate well and focus on the best ideas, but the report also suggests that others might view this as closed-mindedness.

Reflective: Rodney learns from past experiences in a positive manner, but his reflective nature can also inhibit his ability to move forward.

Factual: He is straightforward with a no-nonsense approach to life.

Logical: Rodney has a high level of common sense and takes a logical approach to solving problems.

Controlled: Rodney is very self-disciplined, but being reserved, sometimes misses out on new experiences that could broaden or enrich life.

Retiring: Rodney is modest and quite unassuming, and apt to shy away from attention, conflict and open power struggles, preferring instead to work behind the scenes and minimise friction. However, when he feels it important to take a firm stand on issues that he is passionate about such as getting crewman Chris Davies his MBE, and the fight against the installation of a wind farm in Poole Bay, he stands his ground and nothing will deflect him.

Suspicions: He is often sceptical of quick fixes and new approaches including this Psychometric test. He likes to check things out before making major decisions. This thoroughness is valuable to any quality-centred project but can lead him to become distrustful as to the motives of others.

S Dimension

Change-orientated: Rodney is always looking for novel ideas and innovative solutions, sometimes at the expense of positive aspects of tradition.

Fault-finding: Rodney is good at identifying errors and flaws that others may miss. This is a positive trait when it comes to preparing for a championship, but others have misinterpreted this trait as being nit-picky and cynical.

Spontaneous: Rodney's best ideas invariably come in bursts of inspiration and activity, but he can become frustrated when forced to work within a predictable routine or system.

Frustrated by status quo: Rodney's creativity often follows discontent with the status quo. He will find ways to circumnavigate barriers, which sometimes leads to conflict with higher authority.

Active: He is good at meeting deadlines and completing projects.

C Dimension

Evasive: Rodney will invariably steer clear of personality conflicts and infighting, but his vagueness in these situations can lead to communication breakdowns.

Own person: Rodney is confident in expressing his opinions and will often stand up for himself.

Self-righteous: A hallmark of this trait is the belief that his way is the right way, which is good when it comes to leadership and decisiveness, but others see this as condescending behaviour.

Opinionated: Rodney can articulate firm opinions on a wide range of topics, which is a strength when compromise could lead to defeat or disaster. However, this can also lead to acrimony within a team setting.

Persistent: He works extremely hard to achieve any goal. This is a particular strength within Rodney's character, a point highlighted by Admiral Mike Boyce in his introduction: 'Compromise is not in his vocabulary. In any war situation, Rodney's ruthless single-minded approach – the same qualities that have made him such a successful competitor – would have been invaluable.'

Independent: Rodney operates best on his own without peer pressure or group interactivity, but at times this trait can also lead to a resistance to legitimate feedback from others.

Rigid: Rodney holds himself and others to the highest standards especially when quality outcomes are a necessity. However, this is done occasionally at the expense of flexibility, which can create animosity.

Rodney's motivation

Rodney's developer pattern shows him as an independent thinker who searches for his own solutions. He is always on the lookout for new opportunities and fresh ideas. He thrives on overcoming knotty problems and the chance to scale new heights.

He is inspired by new goals, which often lead to innovative solutions. He will do whatever it takes to succeed, often ignoring conventional thinking.

Rodney's work habits

He is steered by strong will and a high degree of self-reliance. He has great confidence in his own abilities, and in thinking out of the box, he often forges ahead on his own. Rodney does not enjoy group settings and often views collaboration as more a hindrance than help, especially when under pressure to succeed.

He will use his personal sense of power and relentless pursuit of solutions to influence others, and judges the ability of others by his own high standards.

Rodney can use forceful behaviour to get his point across and is used to getting his way. His persistence is one of his chief contributions towards solving problems and he is never overly concerned with the methods employed.

He is not one to give pats on the back and can level heavy criticism on those who don't meet his standards. He can display annoyance when his individualism is limited by group settings, and those on the receiving end of this have labelled him uncaring and belligerent. Similarly, when challenging opportunities evaporate he can become very frustrated.

Insights

Rodney is a strong-willed individual who looks for creative solutions to complex problems. He is most interested in creating new challenges in their purest form. He has strong drive, does not pass the buck and is not afraid to confront difficult issues. At times this can lead to him taking control of situations and forcing his own results on others. He hates the thought of boredom and loss of control, and this makes him very impatient to set new goals and challenges.'

Thanks to John Wiley & Sons for permission to reproduce the DiSC material within this chapter.

TWO

Becoming an Olympian

By 1964 I came to realise that however well I did racing Fireflys and other dinghies, the Navy was never going to give me time off to compete unless I switched to an Olympic class. At that time, there were five Olympic-class boats, only two of which were dinghies. I weighed 10 stone (63.5kg), which was too light for the Finn single-hander, so the only boat I could sail competitively was the Flying Dutchman (FD).

This 20ft (6m) dinghy had been co-designed back in 1951 by two Dutchmen, Conrad Gulcher and naval architect Uus Van Essen, and had won the International Yacht Racing Union (IYRU – now World Sailing) trials to select an international high-performance two-man Olympic dinghy for the 1960 Games in Naples. Other competition included the Osprey, the Hornet, the International 14, the Jollyboat and the Coronet (forerunner of the 505-Class dinghy). Being a restricted, rather strict, one-design class, the FD encouraged constant innovation to maximise performance – making it an ideal Olympic boat and certainly the boat for me.

I had read all about the design but had never actually seen one until Adrian Jardine, a top Army sailor, tipped me off about an FD for sale in Whitstable, where the class had a thriving fleet. Armed with Adrian's flatbed trailer, which I parked discreetly down the road to hide my eagerness, I arrived to find *Flying Phantom* sitting abandoned in a Kent scrap yard. I offered just £220 for her and was amazed to have it accepted. The boat had been locally built by Roy Rigden six years before, but was heavily overweight and with a very unfair hull, and had a tree trunk of a mast, but she was all I could afford. And so I began on a very steep learning curve.

The 1964 British Olympic selection trials were to be held in my home waters in Poole Bay and Mike Boyce – a fellow acting sub-lieutenant in my year at Britannia Royal Naval College at Dartmouth – agreed to crew for me if our captain gave us special leave to attend. Amazingly, the CO granted us ten days in which to prepare and compete in the trials, despite the fact that our passing-out exams would take place only a few weeks later. Mike had very little sailing experience, but was supremely fit, 6ft 3in (1.9m) tall and weighed 12 stone 12lb (81.6kg) – the ideal statistics for an FD crew!

Luckily, I gained permission to keep *Flying Phantom* at Dartmouth, where I devoted a great deal of my spare time to improving her. We sailed her up and down the River Dart, with Mike learning how to trapeze and handle the spinnaker while I got to grips with the various control lines that are part and parcel of an FD, however old and tired she happened to be.

Since we had no opportunity to test ourselves in competition before the Poole Olympic trials, it was no surprise that we didn't do very well. Our one moment of glory came mid-week, when we reached the windward mark first after starting a full minute late having mistimed our return from practising on the course. Everyone else had chosen the inshore route, so I gambled on tacking out to sea simply to do something different. Our moment of fame was all too brief: Keith Musto and Tony Morgan, who went on to win the trials and later the silver medals at the Tokyo Games that year, soon swept past us, followed by much of the fleet, but it was enough to whet my appetite.

Back at Dartmouth, Mike repaid our captain's faith by winning the top prize, the Queen's Sword. It was then clear that nothing was going to stop him from getting to the very top, and he shot up the ranks to command the nuclear submarine *Superb* before not only being promoted to First Sea Lord but ending his naval career at the highest level, becoming Chief of the Defence Staff.

I was a very different kettle of fish. My naval career fast became something of a distraction for what was now another ultimate aim: to win an Olympic gold medal.

After graduating from Dartmouth, I spent my first year at various naval establishments attending sub-lieutenant courses designed to get a feel for what part of the service we wanted to work in. I raced *Flying Phantom* most weekends at Hamble or at open meetings, trying out a number of crews.

It was not all easy going. On one occasion, towing the Dutchman behind my MG TD sports car – bought when I was a midshipman serving in Singapore – my badly modified trailer broke adrift from the hitch. Fortunately it happened at slow speed (the MG being hopelessly underpowered for pulling such a long dinghy) and the boat escaped relatively unscathed. Nevertheless, the event put paid to the weekend racing, instead leading me to meet local boatbuilder Bob Hoare. He did a great job repairing the boat and improving *Flying Phantom* structurally. Little did either of us know then the vital role Bob would play in my Olympic sailing career.

Time aboard HMS *Wakeful*

In 1965, I was posted to the Portsmouth-based frigate HMS *Wakeful*, commanded by Captain David Joel, who, fortunately for me, was also a keen sailor. He gave me every encouragement to pursue my sailing goals, and in a flimsy (a report) sent to the Admiralty, summed me up like this: 'Moody, obstinate and very scruffy – but an utterly brilliant sailor!'

In ports where we made courtesy visits Captain Joel took great delight in challenging other ships and yacht clubs to sailing matches, in which he would ask me and Mike Peaver, a good Finn-Class sailor, to uphold the honour of HMS *Wakeful*. That year, we won every Home Fleet sailing trophy and all the sailing club contests. Someone taking side bets on us would have won a lot of money!

In another report to the Admiralty, Captain Joel predicted: 'Given the time, this man will win a gold medal for Britain at a future Olympic Games.'

He also stood by me when on occasion I ran into trouble. One such incident occurred when, with *Wakeful* spending six months in refit and staffed by a skeleton crew, I found myself as duty officer tasked with mixing and distributing the daily rum issue to the crew. Midway through this, a senior officer appeared and became angry about what he described as an 'unkempt individual distributing the rum ration', and duly reported me. Joel turned a blind eye to this, though his flimsy to the Admiralty about me might well have been in response to this incident.

While *Wakeful* was berthed in Southampton, I moved into a flat above the Rising Sun pub at Warsash with fellow dinghy sailing enthusiasts Patrick King and David Robinson. Coincidentally, Robinson went on to become the Olympic sailing coach of the Royal Yachting Association (RYA) prior to Kiel in 1972.

When my ship finally returned to sea, running out of Portsmouth, Captain Joel assigned me to a Nicholson 32 yacht owned by his friend Sir Philip Beck, then commodore of the Royal Lymington Yacht Club, with orders to deliver her to Bénodet in southern Brittany. We rendezvoused with *Wakeful* off Guernsey to take on board a good supply of her duty-free gin and whisky, then continued to our destination, where Captain Joel and his family were to join the owner for a sailing holiday.

David Joel continued to give me all the time he could to continue my race training and, unknown to me, predicted in one of his many reports to the Admiralty: 'If the Navy had the wit to spare him, Pattisson will go and win a Gold Medal.'

It was comments like this I'm sure that helped me to get the extended time and appropriate appointments needed to concentrate on my Olympic ambitions, and I owe a huge debt of gratitude not only to Captain Joel but also to everyone else for the faith they showed in me.

At a crossroads

By 1967 it was time to choose what branch of the Navy I wanted to specialise in. I elected to join the Fleet Air Arm, partially because of my father's history in the service, but principally because I reckoned flying would give me the best chance of getting time off for racing. I knew from my days at Dartmouth that I suffered from astigmatism in both eyes, limiting my ability to refocus quickly from one object to another. My sister Susan, a trained optician, knew all about this and advised that I could lessen the problem if I exercised my eyes. So, prior to my air medical, I spent considerable time focusing on my index finger, moving it towards and away from my eyes. It worked well, the examining surgeon telling me I had only a slight problem that was not bad enough to stop me from flying. However, just as he was about to pass me fit he had one last flip through my previous medical records from Dartmouth and spotted that I had been failed before because of my eyesight.

'Oh, I see you have already been failed on this before. Sorry, I can't reverse that decision. What if you were to crash an aircraft and kill your observer? I might be blamed. No, I'm afraid you are unfit to fly.'

He wasn't worried that I might be killed too! I was devastated, but in retrospect, that surgeon commander did me a great favour, though it would take me several years to appreciate this.

My second choice was to join the submarine service. I knew there would be a strong possibility of being based at HMS *Dolphin*, just down the road from Hamble River Sailing Club where most of the UK FD crews competed, and I thought I would be free most weekends to continue my racing.

Life at that time was full of trials and tribulations. On one occasion, I took the rare opportunity of a free weekend away from the boat to visit a girlfriend at Weymouth. It was a beautiful morning, the roads were empty and I set out in my lovely MG TD, hood down and feeling very contented. Just a short distance away from home is an angled T-junction with a 'Halt' sign that I had negotiated many times. I was turning left and had a really clear view to the right for several hundred yards. The only vehicle in view was a motorcyclist, driving slowly well in the distance, so I pulled out. Two miles down the road I drew to a stop at traffic lights and the motorcyclist pulled up alongside and said: 'Do you realise you failed to stop at a major Halt sign back there?'

'Did I cause you to brake in any way?' was my retort.

'No,' he said, adding menacingly, 'but you should have stopped.'

As the lights turned green, I made the parting remark: 'So, what's your problem then?' and drove off.

A month later, it became mine!

A traffic summons arrived in the post, and since I had two speeding tickets on my licence already, a third conviction would mean a ban. I had to attend Poole Magistrates' Court and plead my case, which turned on my word against that of the motorcyclist and his wife, who had been riding pillion.

The magistrate asked this witness what he did for a living. 'I'm an amateur traffic observer,' he replied snootily. I was quite peeved, and did my case no good by arguing that the junction didn't need a 'Halt' sign anyway. A 'Give Way' signal was much more appropriate. That cut no ice with the magistrate, who banned me from driving for three months, which was a great inconvenience for my campaign.

Two years later, after our success in Acapulco, Iain and I were invited to a black tie dinner held in our honour in the very same room where that hearing had been held. Among the local dignitaries who attended was, I'm sure, the same magistrate. So, in my speech after receiving commemorative Poole Pottery plates from the Mayor of Poole, I took the opportunity to relate what had happened last time I had been in that room and underlined the effect that a driving ban could have had on our campaign. No one said a word, but some time later, the 'Halt' sign at that junction was downgraded to a 'Give Way' and the junction has remained labelled that way ever since.

Back to 1965. John Oakeley and David Hunt, two of Britain's best-known dinghy sailors, had taken delivery of a new Bob Hoare–built FD named *Shadow*. She was the first from a new mould with a hull shape tweaked by dinghy designer Ian Proctor, Oakeley's boss at Proctor Masts. She had a conventional single-skin hull and relied on self-bailers to remove the bilge water. The pair, who were also based at Hamble River Sailing Club, began to dominate the class, and though we occasionally gave them a run for their money, I knew I was fighting a losing battle with my six-year-old *Flying Phantom*.

I longed for a new boat and finally scraped together the £300 needed to buy a bare shell from the same mould as *Shadow*, including deck and double floor. She was the first to be built with a half double bottom, better described as a raised floor, running from the rear of the centreboard case to the bow, leaving only the back end of the boat as a conventional single-skin floor. Any water entering into the front end of the boat drained out through the centreboard case or through a pair of scupper holes on either side of the hull, neatly eliminating any drag caused by self-bailers. The double floor also made the boat stiffer than *Shadow,* and thanks to Bob Hoare's mastery, the boat finished up still down to minimum weight. As the great Uffa Fox famously said: 'Weight is only any good in a steam roller!'

I built a polythene extension to the garage that would store the 20ft (6m)-long FD, then devoted every spare moment to painstakingly fairing, painting and fitting the dinghy out ready to be named and launched at the start of 1966. The buzzword at the time was 'supercalifragilisticexpialidocious' (meaning 'exceptional'), taken from the catchy song sung by Julie Andrews in the film *Mary Poppins,* and this became the name of my new boat. The artwork, a long multicoloured scrawl, was designed by Elizabeth Baines, an artist friend of my brother's, and I diligently painted the attractive lettering down both sides of the hull.

By now, my naval shore training had come to an end, and I was at sea for the practical side of my submarine training. I was posted to the Oberon-Class sub HMS *Opportune* running 'Perisher' courses (examinations for future submarine captains) off the west coast of Scotland. I still needed to find a suitable crew, and as I was hampered by these extended periods away from home, my brother John, a member of the British University Sailing Team, agreed to act as a recruiting officer.

Worried about the difficulty of finding someone, I also ran an advert in *Yachts and Yachting* magazine:

'WANTED: FD *crew prepared to race mainly Hamble. Bachelor, very strong, extremely fit, experienced helmsman, 6ft 5ins, 13 stone or over preferable. Prepared to share all racing expenses apart from boat already purchased. Ultimate aim MEXICO 1968.'*

It was rather a tall order, and not surprisingly, nobody responded!

John had better luck, persuading Mike Young, a fellow sailing student studying law at the University of London, to join me, and we began training together in *Flying Phantom* in preparation for the planned Olympic qualifying sailing events starting early in 1967.

With a suitable crew now in place, my next task was to negotiate sufficient time off to get both the new boat and us in a competitive position. Life within the submarine service was proving difficult because, even when I did get special leave, this only increased the workload on my four fellow officers on the sub. Very soon it became clear that I had to do something drastic, and so I requested a transfer to another branch of the Navy. That came as quite a shock to my CO, Charles Baker, who, though a keen sailor himself, realised my reasons for wishing to leave submarines.

He sent me before Rear Admiral Ian McGeoch, head of the submarine service, who had quite a reputation, having sunk thousands of tons of Axis shipping in the Mediterranean during World War II. His submarine, HMS *Splendid*, finally succumbed to depth charges dropped by the British-built warship *Hermes* that the Germans had captured from the Greeks. *Splendid* sank to the seabed 500ft (152m) down, where McGeoch blew her air tanks in a practised manoeuvre to raise the submarine to the surface. His crew then abandoned ship through the gun and conning tower hatches while under fire from *Hermes,* which led to 18 of his 48-man crew being killed. McGeoch himself was wounded in the right eye, but stayed aboard the sub until he was sure that there was no one left alive and that she would sink before the enemy could board her.

Although now blind in one eye, McGeoch became a serial escaper. One incident involved digging a tunnel from the Italian hospital he was being treated in. On another occasion, he jumped from a train while being moved between camps, and after being recaptured and taken to Rome for interrogation, he leaped from a moving car in an attempt to seek refuge in the Vatican.

Later, after the Italian armistice, he was promised repatriation, but the Germans commandeered the train he was travelling on. McGeoch was escorted to a prison hospital from which he simply walked away, and after a 400-mile (645km) hike, he eventually crossed the border into neutral Switzerland.

He chose Switzerland – more distant than the Allied front line – because he hoped to seek out Professor Adolphe Franceschetti, who had perfected the use of a strong electromagnet that might draw the jagged sliver of shrapnel from his blind eye.

He was taken with what he called 'the silken dalliance' of Geneva, but eventually became impatient to get home, obtained false papers and walked into France in January 1944. Making contact with the Resistance, he travelled westwards by train and car, then skied across the Pyrenees and into temporary internment in Spain.

From Gibraltar he took passage in the dummy battleship HMS *Centurion,* and his arrival back in Britain was announced to the Resistance by the BBC with the cryptic words '*Le tabac du Petit Pierre est dans la boîte*' – 'Tobacco Petit Pierre is in the box'.

McGeoch was an imposing figure and also a keen yachtsman. As I put my case for leaving the submarine service, he listened, then decided to bargain with me. 'I'll do a deal with you, Pattisson. If you pass your submarine exams, I'll allow you the time off that you need.'

When I did pass those exams a few weeks later, I immediately slapped in a request for time off to compete in various pre-Olympic regattas. Charles Baker, who knew nothing of my bargain, blew his top and stormed off to confront Admiral McGeoch, explaining that he couldn't run his submarine without me.

McGeoch stuck to his side of our deal: 'I've given him my word, so we will have to find a way round this,' he said. And he did – appointing a series of part-time Royal Navy Reserve officers to take my place when I was absent. This still put a huge strain on my fellow officers who had to carry these short-term appointees and I certainly owe them a huge debt of gratitude for the extra work they did in my absence.

Starting out in *Superdocious*

Superdocious, as the new boat quickly became known, was finally ready for her first race at the beginning of 1967. At our first regatta on Grafham Water, Mike and I finished third to class supremos Oakeley and Hunt and 1964 silver medallists Keith Musto and Tony Morgan. It was a good start, and just enough to gain a travel grant to attend international regattas off San Remo and Monaco. However, when it came to organising these first forays abroad I suddenly found myself crewless; Mike's final law exams clashed with these events and brother John had to find a temporary substitute.

Iain MacDonald-Smith, 23 years old, 6ft 3in (1.91m) tall, 12 stone 10lb (81kg), a good helmsman and a fellow member of the university team at Cambridge was, like Mike, also studying law. By pure chance, his exams were a week ahead of those set by the University of London and he was free to join me in San Remo. We hit it off immediately both on the water and off, and we were good enough to challenge Oakeley and Hunt from the very first day we raced together.

Despite being handicapped with an untapered tree-trunk of a mast, borrowed from *Flying Phantom*, we improved as the series progressed to finish third in Monaco. Gina Hunt, wife of John Oakeley's 6ft 4in (1.93m) crewman David, was the principal commentator on the Olympic circuit and had a natural bias towards these European and National champions. She wrote in *Yachting World* magazine:

'So the battle for top British FD intensifies as *Super X* [I hated this shortening of our boat name], *Oliver Twist* [Keith Musto and Tony Morgan] and *Hucklebuck III* [John Truett and Julian Brooke-Houghton] all close the gap on *Shadow*.

Rodney Pattisson got *Super X* going along better and better as the series progressed and by the end was challenging Oakeley quite sternly. Great credit too was due to his crew, Ian MacDonald Smith [misspelled, and the beginning of a lifelong battle to get both our names in print correctly] who had not previously sailed in a Dutchman.'

At the end of the article, Gina Hunt penned a warning:

'There is little doubt that Britain's chance of medals is not high unless more practice is obtained. The Mediterranean is probably the nearest reliable area for light weather practice but the expenses are crippling. Most Continental countries are properly equipped both financially and from a management point of view.

The British outfit is perhaps the last bastion of true amateurism; ill fed, sleeping in the back of cars, generally economising to make ends meet. Even the National and European champions in *Shadow* and the Olympic silver medallists in *Oliver Twist* were given a grant that would only cover their expenses to Dover.

If Britain wants success in the Olympic Games, somebody somewhere should wake up. If the RYA cannot put itself in order then some special arrangements must be made.'

Reading that we had done so well must have been hard on Mike Young, who had shared the work in getting us on to the international circuit. Yet after these two regattas in the Med I felt I was more competitive with Iain and, sadly, had to say goodbye to Mike.

I was determined that we would not fall short of light-air experience, so Iain and I spent the early summer practising hard in preparation for Poole Olympic Week that June. I was again back in home waters and Iain was based most weekends at our family home. As expected, Oakeley and Hunt won a hamperful of silverware, including the British Open Championship title for a second year, and with it the opportunity to represent Britain at Olympic-Class regattas in France and Canada and at the pre-Olympics in Acapulco. However, we were now pushing them hard, winning four of the seven races, including the practice event, to take second place overall. This entitled us to a travel grant to also race at the Expo '67 event in Montreal and later at the pre-Olympics in Acapulco, a year ahead of the Games.

The World Championship in Canada was beset with light winds. Conditions were so fluky that at one point it looked likely that there would not be enough races to constitute the event. Thankfully, though, the winds picked up towards the end and the *Shadow* crew won the World Championship title. Iain and I, meanwhile, were competing in the World Week, racing against many more boats on a separate course, fortunately in a little more wind, and won our event, too.

So, Oakeley and Hunt finished the 1967 season top of the bill, with all three National, European and World Championships to their name. However, to the surprise of many, they didn't fare so well at the pre-Olympic regatta in Acapulco; it was at this last regatta of the year, racing in borrowed boats, that Iain and I finally got the better of them. Had the 100°F (38°C) heat, 85°F (29°C) water temperatures and sweat-inducing humidity been too much for John, who suffered from asthma, or was the *Shadow* crew about to crack?

By contrast, Iain was much more at home in the conditions, having grown up in Africa, and I always loved the heat, sailing in light clothing, often shirtless, with none of that horrible wetsuit itch! On the flip side, the light winds, Pacific swell and complex currents added conundrums to the mix and neither of us did that well. We ended the week 12th overall in an old, hugely overweight Mexican-built boat, and John and David finished 17th in a splendid hired Plastrend boat that had finished second to them in the Worlds.

We arrived home buoyed by the fact that we had really pierced Oakeley and Hunt's armour for the first time, having learned many vital lessons from the venue: the need to be acclimatised, to have a better grasp of the tides and wind patterns, and to have a boat tuned well for the light airs.

I was busy planning significant improvements to *Superdocious* over the following winter months. The most important of these – to replace our tree-trunk mast – had been set in train after the British pre-Olympic regatta in Poole. Helmar Pedersen, the gold medal winner at the 1964 Olympics in Tokyo, had been invited to come over in 1966 from New Zealand by the Royal Yachting Association to provide the British with top foreign competition at the Poole Olympic regatta. Using a borrowed boat, he had brought over his own rig, which included a beautifully tapered mast that was ½in (1.25mm) narrower than that of the Proctor C section that Oakeley and Hunt were using. I knew we had to change the F-section Proctor mast inherited from *Flying Phantom* and was looking for something similar to the much-improved C section sported on *Shadow*. However, Oakeley was sales manager at Proctor, so I was hoping to work with a rival manufacturer and, if possible, produce something even more aerodynamic.

I had been considering a de Havilland spar similar to the one Keith Musto had used to win a silver medal two years before, but Pedersen suggested that the Alspar section, also produced in Australia, was a much better bet. His mast was supported by an elaborate arrangement of crosstrees and spreaders, which presented more windage than one set of spreaders as on *Shadow*. However, I thought the Alspar mast was stiff enough to stand alone and be rigged the same way. I resolved to order one. If it didn't have a Proctor label on it, that alone would worry our rivals.

In those days there was nothing like instant emails or even faxes. My airmail letters to Alspar, penned on flimsy paper, went unanswered and I had no way of knowing if they had received them or not. Luckily, one of my fellow submariners aboard HMS *Opportune* had been seconded to a submarine in Sydney and I gave him the money to order the mast and sit on Alspar's doorstep until they supplied it. He did just this but sadly we then lost contact, and I was never able to thank him for the significant part he played in my Olympic campaign.

It was only through his determination that I finally got a bare section air-freighted to London in time for the start of the 1968 season. The mast arrived damaged, with the top 4in (10cm) of the tapered section badly kinked. Rather than showing my hand to John Oakeley at Proctor Masts, I took it to John Powell at rival mast manufacturer Sparlight, who agreed to administer surgery, and helped us to rig it using single spreaders – just as *Shadow*'s spar was set up. Additionally, we carefully faired the edges of the spreader roots and sheave blocks into the section using car body filler to minimise wind resistance.

At this time, I was posted to HMS *Tiptoe*, the oldest submarine in the Navy, then commanded by Lieutenant Commander Robin Whiteside, who, fortunately for me, was also supportive of my campaign. He even arranged for *Superdocious* to be stored in a Nissen hut at our base at HMS *Dolphin* so that I could continue to work on her. He also encouraged my fellow officers to share my duties between them when they were one man down at sea, and they share the plaudits because without the time they allowed me to train, I doubt if I would have succeeded.

One major advance at that time was the fitting of a spinnaker chute pioneered by the Green brothers from Canada. Roger Green had come over to take delivery of a new Hoare boat and to compete in the 1967 Poole Bay regatta. We trialled with each other prior to that event and became good friends. I saw just how well his spinnaker system worked, and having brought over a spare moulding, he gave it to me and I got Bob Hoare to fit it in secret to *Superdocious* over the winter.

Oakeley and Hunt, who had a near-perfect routine for setting and recovering their spinnaker from a bag set to one side of the mast, poured scorn on the idea. They thought that a heavy, wet spinnaker sitting in the front of the boat and the water that would enter the chute over the bow would affect boat speed, but with sensible drainage holes in the bottom of the spinnaker sock and the sail pulled well back in the boat, this was never a problem.

However proficient the *Shadow* crew were at setting and retrieving their spinnaker, David still had to come into the boat, first to hoist the sail, and again to repack it in its bag, whereas Iain could stay out on the wire when I was hoisting and retrieving the sail, giving us a valuable edge at the start and finish of these downwind and reaching legs.

We also realised the need to be extremely fit. Iain, who by now was articled to a firm of solicitors in London, hated the thought of running on the beach with me, but did a lot of swimming and signed up with Al Murray's gym near St Paul's. Al was one of the greatest weightlifting coaches in the world and devised a set of exercises to strengthen his back muscles – a great help to him when it came to coping with the thick towelling weight jacket he had to wear when hanging out on the trapeze wire for most of the race.

Our first test with the new Alspar mast and spinnaker chute came at the Grafham Indicator trials at the start of the 1968 season. We won all four races, in varying conditions, with ease from Keith Musto and Tony Morgan's new boat *Oliver Twist*. Gina Hunt blamed Oakeley and Hunt's lacklustre performance on the fact that they had made no improvements to *Shadow* for eight months, preferring to wait and see how the competition was shaping up before instigating any changes themselves.

Our new mast worried Hunt. He was an engineering professor at the University of Southampton and had developed most of the systems on *Shadow*. But with Oakeley tied to using Proctor-branded spars there was no way they could be seen racing with an Alspar mast, and anyway, it was now too late to get one from Australia tuned up in time for the Olympic trials in June.

We were just as consistent at the Open Championship in Whitstable, taking two firsts and three second placings, while our

Shadow opponents were testing out a variety of masts, including one wrapped in carbon – a new, exotic material that had just appeared on the scene. They also had a brilliantly made titanium centreboard, but all failed to rekindle their form.

The story was repeated at the San Remo Easter regatta. We counted three firsts, two seconds and two third placings within the 80-strong fleet, and even Gina Hunt's commentaries in the press now began to show a grudging appreciation of our speed.

And then came the final do-or-die Olympic trials back in Poole Bay. Before the series, I borrowed a friend's speedboat and spent a day checking the tidal stream and direction around the course area by laying a series of small marks and measuring the movement with a tidal stick at half-hourly intervals. It was all immensely useful, but I must have forgotten to pick up one of the marks, for the following week I read a press article suggesting that someone had tried to sabotage the weekend's powerboat racing with an anchored line designed to snag propellers. I kept my own counsel on that one!

I had also been working on developing a secret centreboard with a trim tab on the trailing edge designed to increase lift and reduce leeway. Just as I was checking its legality with Vernon Forster, the IYRU's chief measurer, who should walk into the measuring tent but yachting correspondent Jack Knights. He was competing in the Finn-Class single-hander trials and spotted the significance of our board immediately. I pleaded with him not to reveal our secret at least until after the Olympics, but seeing a scoop, he took no notice and wrote up a full account of the hinged foil in his column in the next issue of *Yachts & Yachting* magazine. I cursed him for letting the cat out of the bag, and four months later Ulli Libor, our German rival at Acapulco, turned up with a similar development. By then we were using a Mark 2 board that was significantly better, but the incident showed how difficult it was to keep developments away from the prying eyes of the press, even in off-limit areas like the measurer's tent.

That incident was really annoying, and made me determined to get my own back on old Jack. My opportunity came during the 1969 World Championships in Naples when he asked me to explain a system we had fitted to adjust the mast shrouds using kicking strap winches fitted under the side decks. The dummy I sold him was taken hook, line and sinker! I said it gave us the ability to lean the mast to weather and was the secret to us pointing higher to windward than anyone else. All was revealed in his next magazine column and we laughed at the thought of all our rivals trying to do the same.

Kiel Olympic Week was followed shortly after by the European Championship on Lake Balaton, Hungary, a few weeks before the final UK selection trials in Poole. All our foreign competition were at the German event, so it was important to be present. My results weren't bad but I had noticed a slight loss in pointing ability and discovered water had leaked into one side of the double bottom. We eventually traced this to a small split in the centreboard case. With the Hungarian event only days away, Ulli Libor, my good friend and German rival, came to my aid, inviting me to stay at his house in Hamburg while Hein, his FD builder, repaired my boat.

He did a brilliant job of gluing, pinning and bolting the side of the case back together, but one morning I arrived at his yard earlier than usual to view progress and was surprised to find my boat upside down with all the measurement templates laid on her. Hein was obviously taking the opportunity to compare the shape of this Bob Hoare hull with his own moulding, and since he didn't charge me for the repair, I had to take it as fair recompense for the job he had done and for Ulli's generous hospitality. What more could I say?

Back in 1968, Hungary was still in the Eastern Bloc and to help our cash flow, I agreed in Kiel to sell a genoa to one of the Hungarian FD crews, who was to pay us in forints when we arrived. I had gained special permission from the Navy to cross through the Iron Curtain and was told to keep my eyes open for any military activity and to expect a thorough debrief on my return. I was also warned about being entrapped in a compromising situation, but, taken with the prospect of advances from pretty women, Iain was delighted with the idea of swapping names with me for the week and seeing what happened. He took this quite literally, and before the championship started, took all the cash and my car one night to drive to a party in Budapest. I was furious. He left me with no money to buy dinner for myself and so I locked him out of the apartment. We were still not speaking the following morning and Oakeley and Hunt sensed the tension between us immediately. This, they thought, was their chance, and they did all they could to aggravate the situation further. Fortunately, this failed and I used this first race to try out a new genoa. *Superdocious* simply shot away to win by a large margin, and by the time we had crossed the finish line the two of us were the best of friends again.

We dominated that week and went on to win five out of six races, winning the UK Olympic trials with a race to spare. John and David came second in *Shadow*, and so they joined us at the Mexico Olympics, but only as our tune-up crew.

Vernon Stratton – who had represented Britain in the Finn Class at the 1964 Olympics in Tokyo – was to be the British Team Manager, ably assisted by his wife Peppy; both were to become lifelong friends. Vernon owned a successful advertising agency and handled not only the practicalities of the Olympic team, but also the entire PR side, keeping the press at arm's length.

Having beaten the current World and European Champions for our place at Acapulco, we were seen by the media as likely medal winners and as such became the subject of continuous requests for interviews. The last thing I wanted was the additional pressure of being put on a plinth of certainty, and Vernon, by and large, kept us out of the media spotlight.

We spent the rest of the period prior to Mexico training in Poole Bay, two-boat trialling with other FD crews, including Oakeley and Hunt, testing different rig and sail combinations. Sailmakers could see the commercial kudos of having their labels on our sails and Musto & Hyde, Bruce Banks and Seahorse vied to develop the best mainsail, genoa and spinnakers for particular conditions. Each sail was rigorously tested in various wind ranges, first on *Superdocious* and then swapped with whatever sail the trial boat was using to double-check our findings.

We developed two fixed lightweight rudders and several centreboards with varying aerofoil sections. The profile and thickness of the FD board is strictly controlled, but I produced a Mark II version of my compromised trim tab board, which proved to be a big improvement on the original.

I have been a strong believer in the principle behind the gybing centreboard to create extra lift ever since mastering the science on my old Firefly *Ismene* No 27. By far the oldest boat in the fleet, she had her original aluminium decks and buoyancy tanks when I bought her, so I used a kit of plywood parts from builders Fairey Marine to upgrade the boat to a Mk II version. The kit also included a transom, which strangely had a slightly different profile to the original, but fearing this might change the shape of the hull and affect the boat's acknowledged performance, I never changed this.

The problem with the standard Firefly was that the centreplate, cut from steel or aluminium sheet, was locked centrally at the front of the case by a bush set on either side at the pivot point. The trailing edge, however, was free to slop from side to side in the case. By removing the front bushes and adding small pieces of wood to the slot in line with the trailing edge of the plate in its downward position, you could reverse the angle so that the plate produced positive lift, and so reduce leeway rather than enhance it, as the standard arrangement stupidly did.

My simple modification worked very effectively in helping *Ismene* point higher into wind than other Fireflys, as I was to prove at Herne Bay during the 1965 Sir Ralph Gore Trophy, the principal race during the Firefly National Championships. I was leading by a full leg of the course when the winds blew up so strongly that the diamonds on my old metal mast snapped and I was dismasted, along with 20 others who were also forced to retire. The race was abandoned, and after returning ashore, something of a witch-hunt developed, with race officials checking the centreplate case of every boat. Was a gybing board in a true one-design boat legal or not? I didn't have time to find out. The Navy had released me for just the one day to compete in this special race, and I was already on my way back to my Gosport submarine base.

The following year, brother John maintained family honour by winning the National Championship at Felixstowe, with five straight victories. He was just 18 and the youngest ever to claim the trophy – without, I guess, the help of a gybing board!

Some years later, I had the pleasure of meeting Uffa Fox, designer of the Firefly and many other remarkable boats. When

I explained the advantages of a gybing plate in the Firefly dinghy he remained sceptical, partially I guess because the offending bushes were not something he had shown on the original drawings, but had been included by Fairey Marine, probably without his knowledge.

Gearing up for the Games

Back to 1968, and Owen Aisher, chairman of the Royal Yachting Association and a keen yachtsman, whose son Robin had also won selection to the British Olympic sailing team in the 5.5 keelboat class, asked if there was anything we needed for our boat. We had numerous sails to cover every eventuality, we had our special Alspar mast, Helmsman Paints had applied their new super-smooth graphite coating Graphspeed to the hull bottom, and we already had a couple of other tricks up our sleeve to psych out our competition once we got to Acapulco. After a lot of thought, I wondered about replicating a miniature version of the 'Park Avenue' boom sported on the 1930 US America's Cup defender *Enterprise*. Owen agreed to fund this, and John Powell at Sparlight masts fabricated it for me.

This 5in (15cm)-deep triangular boom was light in construction and extremely stiff, provided an end-plate effect to the bottom end of the mainsail and, most importantly, added the equivalent of 5sq ft (0.46sq m) of extra sail area when sailing downwind. The one problem with it was that it gave Iain less headroom to get across the boat when tacking and gybing, but he soon got used to that. It became another secret weapon in our arsenal for Acapulco that Jack Knights hadn't seen, and to ward off potential protests from rival camps I got John Powell to make up a 5in (15cm)-diameter template – the maximum allowed within the rules – to prove that the boom could pass through it.

I've always tried to keep a low profile, particularly with the press, but before we packed *Superdocious* up to be shipped to Mexico, Vernon Stratton asked Iain and me to do a photo shoot with Eileen Ramsay, then one of Britain's top sailing portrait photographers. This was not something I was keen on, because any pictures published before the Games could give our rivals vital intelligence about our boat and its set-up. We won an assurance from Eileen that she would not release any of the shots until after the Olympics. We went out as far as Old Harry Rocks off Studland and sailed around her stationary launch. The pictures she took of us were not only the best we had seen, but also probably the most widely published pictures Eileen had ever taken. They appeared everywhere because so few pictures were taken of us racing in Acapulco, and she had an 'exclusive'!

After the trials I returned to duty aboard HMS *Tiptoe* and soon realised that the foul-smelling air and smoke – nearly everyone smoked on board – was having an adverse affect on my ability to keep fit. To their credit, the Top Brass agreed to give me a month's leave to acclimatise to the hot and humid conditions expected in Acapulco. Once *Superdocious* and *Shadow* were on their way by ship to Mexico, my brother John and I quietly took off in my Morgan to tour round the hot spots of Spain to continue my running routine and get my system used to foreign food.

Vernon Stratton persuaded the RYA to fund the team's arrival in Mexico five weeks before the Games in order to get fully acclimatised. He also brought out David Houghton, a keen sailor and weather guru seconded from Britain's National Weather Centre at Bracknell. David did a brilliant job, setting off his weather balloons each day to build a detailed picture of the microclimate within Acapulco Bay, and since no other team had anyone near his calibre of expertise, this became another arrow to our bow. David's detailed explanations certainly unravelled much of the mystery surrounding the light, fluky winds that were to prevail.

Quite by chance, Vernon came across a British pilot, a keen sailor, who had been given time off by his boss to fly down to Acapulco in the company plane to watch the Olympic regatta. He agreed to fly over the courses each morning and plot the lines of currents on a chart we gave him, before placing it in a plastic bottle and tossing it out of the plane window to land close to our support inflatable shortly before our starts. This became vital information since Acapulco was experiencing thunderstorms most nights that led to unusual torrential downpours. Floodwater came pouring into the bay from the rivers, and the lighter colour of the fresh water against the dark blue Pacific stream was clearly visible from the air. Crucially, this floodwater was considerably warmer than the sea and, being the top layer, was driven by the wind in a different direction to the steady ocean current.

No other teams had any support at all, so this, coupled with David Houghton's accurate weather forecasts each morning, gave us a considerable advantage.

Ashore, *Superdocious* attracted much attention even before the start of the Olympic regatta. As we had won races by such large margins prior to the Games, some of our rivals were convinced that we must be cheating in some way. There was outcry when our trim tab centreboard was submitted for measurement. The measurer passed it as legal within class rules, but the Olympic Jury made their own ruling, banning it on the grounds that my development of it represented an unfair advantage over poorer nations – a rule I had never heard of before or since. Such was the power of the jury. But it didn't matter much because I was more than happy with the performance of our normal gybing board, which anyway seemed to give us the ability to outpoint every other boat in the fleet.

Two days before the practice race we revealed our miniaturised electrical wind indicator produced by B&G. This led to another flurry of protests and a meeting of the jury. The analogue display was powered by a 9-volt battery, which rivals claimed was 'stored energy', and, as such, against the rules. David Hunt went into the protest hearing on our behalf and argued successfully that the indicator was no different to the battery-powered stopwatches that many relied on to time their race starts. The issue led to considerable discussion and, just as I hoped, distracted some of our rivals from their own preparations while we quietly got on with the job in hand. The gadget did offer a practical advantage because it put an end to staring up into the glare of the sun to see the wind indicator at the top of the mast. Instead, I could read the display at deck level while looking ahead at the waves and sea state. It also provided an instant indication of apparent wind direction when the boat accelerated down the Pacific swells. Admittedly, the kit added around 2lb (900g) to the overall weight of the boat, but the psychological advantage far outweighed this.

The 'Park Avenue' boom, also kept under wraps until just before the regatta, caused equal disquiet, but no one could argue after seeing the spar pass easily through the 5in (15cm)-diameter measurement template we had brought with us.

The Flying Dutchman fleet was to be based on floating pontoons covered with carpeting to allow the boats to be slid on and off easily. I was not at all happy with this because there was no room to roll *Superdocious* over on her side to shackle the head of the mainsail to the top of the mast. The FD rules insist that the mast must be buoyant, and since there was very little room within the small luff groove of the Alspar mast for three halyards, jib, spinnaker and main, we had dispensed with the wire main halyard altogether. After a lot of negotiating, Vernon Stratton gained permission for us to keep *Superdocious* on a launching trolley ashore, which got our rivals running for their rulebooks once more. There had to be something in there specifying a main halyard. No, there wasn't, and not having one saved the 2lb (900g) in weight that the wind indicator had added. This simply fuelled further suspicions that we were hiding something and led to calls for *Superdocious* to be remeasured. Vernon Forster, the chief measurer, would have none of it. 'She has passed measurement and is a legal Flying Dutchman,' he declared firmly.

Concerned about the growing unrest over our boat, the organisers posted an armed guard to stand alongside *Superdocious* each night to deter anyone from trying to sabotage her, but this simply fed suspicions further. We didn't mind. The more time our rivals spent worrying about us, the less they spent on their own game.

Vernon secured one other big advantage over the other teams – the exclusive use of a fast inflatable boat. For everyone else, it took a good hour or more to be towed out to the course strung out behind the official Bertram 25 powerboats in the full glare of the sun. Vernon, with his powerful outboard, could get us out there and back again after the race within 15 minutes. He also carried our spare sails, tools, lines and an emergency outboard because I'm sure the tow boats would have refused to throw us a line had we broken down!

Weed was another problem in Acapulco Bay. It didn't matter so much when it wrapped itself around the centreboard because we could clear the weed by raising and lowering the centreboard momentarily, but once it had got caught on our fixed rudder it became very difficult to cast off. I spent hours setting razor blades into the leading edge of the blade only to find that we rarely went fast enough to produce the knife-edge effect required to slice through the weed. We finally came up with a sail batten 'weed' stick with a V-shaped wire fashioned from a coat hanger to slide down the leading edge and push the weed off. The system worked well, and since I didn't see anyone else employing anything similar, we kept our stick well hidden inside the double bottom away from prying eyes when we were back on shore.

The contentious first race

By the time of the first race, Iain and I were not only the youngest and fittest competitors within the FD fleet, but the lightest too. We had embarked on a high protein diet as soon as we arrived in Mexico and both of us lost 1 stone (6.35kg) in weight before reverting to a normal diet three days before the start. Saving 2 stone (12.7kg) of all-up weight had a greater effect on our performance than anything the wind indicator, the Park Avenue boom or even our gybing centreboard could contribute, for this lower weight helped us to be the first up on the plane on the Pacific swell, allowing us to sail much deeper downwind.

The first race, however, did not go as planned. The race officer did not give himself time to get organised. The naval vessel acting as committee boat and the mark at the pin end of the line were both anchored to 70m lines and not easy to reposition. As a result, the start line, which was ridiculously long, was set with a 25-degree bias to port, which, combined with the adverse current, made it almost impossible to start on starboard (the right-of-way tack) and clear the line. The race officer should have abandoned the start and relaid the line, but he let the fleet go, which led to chaotic scenes at the pin end of the line and several collisions.

We held back, hoping to tack on to port as soon as possible, but everyone else had the same idea and there wasn't room for all. Amid this melee, the Green brothers from Canada caught us on port tack. This was the pair we had trialled with prior to the Olympic selection trials back in Poole; they had enjoyed my family's hospitality at home and we had traded ideas about boat speed. I thought they were friends but quickly found, when they sought our disqualification at the end of the race, that friends don't exist on the water in Olympic competition.

We put in a short port tack but were back on starboard by the time they came close. Roger then luffed head into wind and our gunwales came together, and by the time we untangled ourselves, both boats were tail-end Charlies.

I was furious. This was the biggest race of our lives. I learned a hard lesson that day – something I was able to impart to a young Ben Ainslie when he started out on his long road to Olympic success.

Despite this, Iain and I quickly got back into our stride: the conditions were perfect, and slowly but surely we recovered the situation, sweeping through the 29-strong fleet to take the winning gun by nearly three minutes.

Back at the dock, however, our victory smiles were short-lived. The Greens found no shortage of crews as keen as them to see us disqualified, and lined them up to testify against us.

We turned to the jury, whose boat had been positioned close to the incident, to verify our story, but like wise monkeys, none had seen, heard or spoken about it. At the protest hearing, though, we learned that a photographer and a film cameraman stationed on the jury boat had photographed the clash. We also found that the black-and-white prints produced for the hearing had been presented in the wrong order, crucially distorting the chronology of the collision as a result.

We were disqualified from the race, a grossly unfair ruling that Vernon Stratton set out to right. He located the photographer to confirm the true order of the pictures, and arranged with our British pilot friend to fly the TV footage up to Mexico City to get it developed overnight. This footage confirmed our side of events – that we were not to blame for the collision – but the chairman of the jury refused to even consider a rehearing, let alone view this new evidence.

Sports writer Hugh McIlvanney came down hard on the Olympic organisers. Writing in the *Observer* newspaper that next Sunday, he first set the scene and soon after was quoting Vernon Stratton:

'If that disqualification in the first race costs Rodney and Iain the Gold, it will be a grotesque injustice.

Stratton's refusal to accept the Protest Committee's ruling is the result of painstaking investigation conducted after he had learned that their findings had been based partly on photographic evidence. "If they hadn't introduced the pictures, we should have had no option but to accept their decision without question." Stratton swiftly established that the pictures passed around the committee had been numbered wrongly and the chronology of the collision incident was crucially distorted.

The case against Pattisson as helmsman of Superdocious was essentially that he precipitated the bump at the start by being on port (give way) tack. Stratton's enlarged photographs convinced me that Pattisson, having tacked to port, was back on starboard some time before his boat became entangled with Green's. That meant that Green should have given way to him.

The pictures certainly refute the Canadian's testimony that the course taken by Superdocious forced him to go head-to-wind. And they indicate that the Canadian and New Zealand witnesses who supported Green were in no position to contribute reliable accounts of what happened.

All this permanent evidence is duplicated in a cine-film of the race. Having heard a whisper about the existence of the film, Stratton tracked down its owner, and then flew to Mexico City to have it processed with the help of an English television unit. Though naturally glad of the confirmation provided by the film, he says he would not need to prove to the committee (on which the United States, Mexico, Greece, Portugal and Japan had members) that a disastrous error has been made.

"The stills would be enough to show that Rodney and Iain were blameless. I'm not interested in having the Canadian penalised but I am convinced now that he had made up his mind to force Rod and Iain on the wrong side of the marker at the start. My file of pictures shows that *they were dragged back to the very rear of the fleet. Yet they were sixth at the end of the first beat, and eventually won easily."*

Pattisson has a simple explanation of that incredible recovery. "Iain said 'Forget it, let's sail.' So we sailed." But it required even more resilience to emerge unshaken from the squabble that surrounded the disqualification, a psychological strength that persuaded many neutral observers in Acapulco that the British pair could achieve the unique feat of winning all seven races. They went into the water today burdened with the knowledge that they had to do exactly that to be sure of the gold medal.

Each team is allowed to discard one performance, but that initial fiasco means that Pattisson and MacDonald-Smith might be shattered by one indifferent result because the German Ulrich Libor was awarded the first race and followed up with two seconds and a third.

"I lie awake at nights imagining what would happen if the German decided to forget about himself in the last race and concentrate on ruining Rodney's chances," says Stratton. "He could go close to the wrong side of the markers at the start, get Rodney, and take his wind throughout the race. He could just stay with him, taking his wind all the time, tacking to shut him out."

Disqualification wouldn't matter to the German if he knew he had six reasonable performances and Rodney was only going to have five good ones. Everybody tells me that he is not the kind of chap to do this, but you can never tell. In any case, our boys could have their rudder broken at the start or have some unlucky accident. That's why you are allowed one discard. Now theirs has been taken away from them. Some of these officials seem to think it's not a bad thing – they reckon it gives the other fellows a more sporting chance. They don't realise how much this means to Rodney and Iain, how much dedication and sacrifice has gone into their effort to win here.

"Success in this standard of competition is mainly a massive cumulative attention to detail. Superdocious is the most gadgety boat in the event, but all the gadgets are bloody useful. They all do a job. Even after winning our trials easily, Rodney was ready to start all over again on improvements. He fitted an apparent wind indicator like that carried on 12 metre yachts and ocean racers, and it is a great advantage. It added two pounds to the weight in the boat, but he saved

2lb by quite radically removing the wire main halyard. That's the way he works."

Yesterday was one day that Pattisson did not have to work. It was the single break in the long week of racing and he spent it at a beach party on an island opposite the luxurious hotel where the British yachtsmen are lodged. Their living conditions (iced Cuba Libres on the verandas of penthouse suites) make a disconcerting contrast with the army-style existence of the athletes crowded into the bare blocks of the Olympic village here in Mexico City. On the way to the island, the handsome Negro boatman pointed out the homes of John Wayne and Hedy Lamarr squatting insecurely on the wooded cliffs, interrupting his commentary to suck down oysters freshly plucked from the seabed by the divers who followed us. The spartan demands of Olympic competition seemed unutterably remote and were made even more so by the sight of Pattisson lolling on a beach chair among pretty girls. But the tanned body was lean and hard, and the eyes, set deep beneath the blond hair, had the preoccupied look of a determined man under prolonged pressure.

Pattisson is the polite, rather shy son of an advertising man from Poole, but he is as tough and self-sufficient as a Royal Navy submarine officer is expected to be. "I may not be really fit compared to some of the track men," he said quietly, watching his bare foot scoop trenches in the sand. "But Iain and I are strong enough to stand two to three hours out there in the middle of the bay and still be able to think fast and clearly at the end of a race. Iain's hanging out on the wire much of the time, with his feet on the gunwale, holding on to 90 square feet of genoa, and that's not an exercise for boys.

"But crouching in the boat in the really light winds takes a terrible toll, too. You can't stretch, and unless you are really in shape, your mind stiffens up along with your body. It was to get the fitness needed for that sort of situation that I gave up drinking last year. I was a moderate drinker by Navy standards but that still means you sink a few, rather too many for this game.

"But I don't believe in a monastic life, early to bed, and all that stuff. I like to get out and relax after a race, have a good meal and maybe go dancing with a girlfriend until after midnight. On patrol in submarines we get only four hours' sleep so if I get about seven here it is no trouble *to get up at eight and go for a half hour run. Iain and I are both in our early 20s and we won't be beaten for fitness.*

"We don't want to be beaten for anything but it is a dreadful strain knowing that we can't afford a single slip. The thought of it inhibits us all the time. On Thursday, we knew exactly where we wanted to start, but there was a bunch of boats there so we couldn't risk it. We ended up giving the others 30 seconds' start. It worked out all right because we had plenty of room to tack as we wanted. We finished the first of the three beats very well placed and went on to win by three minutes, but who is to say it will always go that way?"

As it happened, quite a few people in the party were willing to bet that it would always go that way, at least during the Olympic races if the breezes drop appreciably below the present level of Force 2 to 4, increasing the element of chance produced by their constant changes of direction and the unreliable currents created when warm water slides over the cool tides from the ocean – then even the British team's magnificent meteorological organisation may not save Pattisson and MacDonald-Smith from severe difficulties.

But at this moment, the odds are that Britain will provide the longest name on the honours list.'

I was deeply annoyed, but Iain took a more sanguine view. 'Look, we pulled through from last to first. We have the speed. We just have to keep it up for the rest of the regatta.'

He was right of course and the rest of the British team closed ranks around us, encouraging Iain and me to go out to repeat that first win. I found it hard to put it out of my mind – this disqualification would have to be our discard race, leaving no room for further errors – but I became determined not to allow this injustice to affect our performance.

Going for gold

In the second race we underlined our superior performance, leading from start to finish, and we continued to point higher and sail faster to win four more races with equal ease. In the final race, we had only to finish to secure gold. This we did, starting last from the leeward end of another heavily biased line, and carrying a spare rudder and genoa on board for safe measure. Such was our speed advantage that *Superdocious* pulled right through the fleet and would have won this race too had a wind shift on the final beat not relegated us to second. We ended the series with a DSQ, 1st, 1st, 1st, 1st, 1st, 2nd, to finish the Olympic regatta with the lowest recorded score – a record that stands to this day!

A shift in the goalposts

Our performance had global repercussions: the International Olympic Committee (IOC) banned the use of planes overflying the regatta area at future Games, and the Flying Dutchman Class outlawed articulating centreboards and tightened up the measurement rules to such an extent that *Superdocious* and other Bob Hoare–built boats became out of class. *Superdocious* had to go back to Bob Hoare and have additional veneers glued along the turn of bilge to meet the new measurement criteria, which made her overweight and the hull less fair. Bob also stripped off the beautiful mahogany decks and replaced them with lighter gaboon plywood.

More positively, moves were made to 'professionalise' the race management at future Olympic regattas with experienced sailors who knew how to set a start line fairly and with jury members who would take their responsibilities more seriously. At Acapulco, we got the sense that the jury felt that they were a law unto themselves rather than being there to administer the rules justly.

Questions were also starting to be raised about my own 'amateur' status. Both subjects were covered in a letter to the *Daily Telegraph* written by Sir Atholl Oakeley, the father of John, and one of the last to receive a hereditary peerage, for his contribution to the sport of wrestling. He wrote: 'Competitors compete as individuals for the amateur championship of the World. No other placing is of any importance.'

In a clear dig at me, he added:

'It is no use complaining that competitors, sent by other Countries, are in reality professionals through being excused all work prior to the trials, when England does the same thing (in at least one case) for months

beforehand to the detriment of bona fide, 100 per cent, amateurs who [as I had to] have to work for their living.

This point, and that referees should be appointed from ex-professional champions (such as Tunney, Dempsey, Marciano and Clay for boxing and Jack Sherry, Assirati, Sherman and myself for wrestling) might well, if adopted, do away with much of the criticism levelled against the modern Olympiad.'

Once back home, the Royal Navy had me back in uniform attending various PR functions, and it was at one of these receptions that I let slip the conundrum I was wrestling with: to return to the Navy as a serving naval officer on submarines or to accept offers to steer a series of top-level yachts in competitions around the world. A guest at one of these luncheons addressed the subject and I answered his questions a little too candidly. Later, I got a call from a news reporter asking the same questions. Since neither the Navy nor the RYA had thought to provide any media training, I did not recognise that he was fishing for a story and that I should have refused to speak to him. Instead, I gave him straight answers. To my horror, and doubtless that of the top brass in Whitehall, the headline in the *Daily Mail* the next morning screamed out: 'Olympic sailor's problem – NO TIME FOR THE NAVY'.

The story ran:

'Lieut. Rodney Pattisson, who won a sailing gold medal for Britain at the Mexico Olympics last month, is thinking of leaving the Royal Navy, which he joined when he went to Dartmouth almost ten years ago.

Since his success with Superdocious, *25 year-old Pattisson has received several offers to act as helmsman in yachts competing for the Admiral's Cup next year. And now he feels torn between his life in the Navy – which he loves – and the sport, which has won him such wide acclaim.*

"The one thing I will never give up is my sailing," he said yesterday… "If I find that it is just not possible for me to have sufficient time off to follow this sport, then regrettably, I will have to offer my resignation."'

The story really upset me. I owed the Royal Navy a great deal and I should have been more diplomatic. But it was out and no doubt led to consternation in some circles, though Captain David Joel attempted to come to my aid with a suggestion to the Admiralty for a recruitment advert: 'Join the Royal Navy: Sail and win a Gold Medal!'

Sadly, that didn't go down with the Top Brass any better than the article.

Thankfully, my comments did not affect our inclusion in the 1969 New Year honours list. Harold Wilson's Labour government set a precedent that year by awarding all gold medallists, in both single and team events, with Member of the Order of the British Empire – MBE – medals. Fleet Street and yachting magazine editors also voted Iain and me as British Yachtsmen of the Year. Iain and I decided to stay as a team for another year to press home our performance advantage within the FD Class and try to wrest the world title from Oakeley and Hunt. We retained our European title and went on to win the World Championship in Naples, taking the title with five straight victories, before I decided to try my hand at offshore racing, steering for Ulli Libor's German production boat entry *Listang* in the 1969 Quarter Ton Cup, which also ended with overall honours.

With the 1970 FD World Championship being held in Adelaide early into the new year, I agreed to steer Sir Max Aitken's yacht, *Crusade*, in the 1969 Sydney–Hobart Yacht Race, which turned into something of a cliffhanger. This was to be my first experience in long offshore racing, and it was certainly exciting, with us just beating Alan Bond's *Apollo* to line honours by 5 minutes at the end of this 608-mile (1,126km) ocean classic. While waiting for *Superdocious* to arrive in Adelaide by ship, I teamed up with Australian yacht designer Scott Kaufman to race in the Australian Soling championship in Melbourne. We were sailing a boat loaned to us by Mike Kumm, whose son volunteered to be our third man. We had not raced together before, and it showed during that first race, so I had us stay out to practise our spinnaker setting and gybing until we got the routines right, and we went on to win the championship. The 1970 FD World Championship in Australia was to be our swansong. Iain now had his heart set on campaigning a Finn single-hander for the 1972 Olympics, so it was important to both of us that we ended this partnership on a high. We retained our crown, and in May 1973 had one last sail together in our original *Superdocious*. Dunhill contributed hugely to British Olympic sailing in 1968 and 1972 and it was a fitting and final contribution when they purchased the boat, by now no longer competitive, and donated her to the National Maritime Museum at Greenwich. Iain and I sadly rigged her for this last sail down the Thames, and even now, almost five decades later, she remains on view at the National Maritime Museum Cornwall for all to see, and hopefully to encourage others.

Iain MacDonald-Smith on Rodney

'The major contrast between Rodney and successful Olympians today such as Ben Ainslie lies in the modern training methods now used to bring sailors to peak form. Ben has been coached all his life, while Rodney was self-taught and to a large extent self-funded. Ben and others are the product of an elite training squad system that has had massive financial support from the Lottery Fund. This has paid for the latest sports sciences – fitness, nutrition and medical – together with a research and development department working behind the scenes to discover and develop new and better ways of doing things.

Behind every gold medal is a technical story, and for us it was the Alspar mast that gave us the breakthrough we needed to beat the World Champions for the Olympic berth. Without that new mast, there is little doubt that we would have finished second in the UK Olympic trials. The Flying Dutchman suited Rodney. Unlike strict one-design classes such as the Firefly, the wide tolerances and open attitude to development allowed him room to experiment. The class also had a great UK dynasty: Keith Musto and Tony Morgan, silver medallists at the 1964 Games; Dick Pitcher and Ian McCormack, World Champions in 1965; John Oakeley and

David Hunt, World Champions in 1967; Doug Bishop and Dave Rayment, Hornet World Champions in 1967 and 1968; and Larry Marks, a multiple 505 World Champion.

Rodney was fastidious with everything, whether it be fairing the hull, putting a perfect finish to the foils or minimising windage around the rig. Preparing *Superdocious* in Montreal for the Worlds Week, we found weed to be a particular hazard. It didn't matter so much when it wrapped itself around the centreboard because we could clear it by raising and lowering it momentarily, but once weed had got caught on the rudder, it became very difficult to cast off. Rodney spent hours setting razor blades into the leading edge of the foil and was incandescent when he found that we rarely went fast enough to slice through the weed. Undaunted by the time wasted, he then came up with a "weed stick" made from a sail batten with V-shaped wire fashioned from a coat hanger attached to the bottom end, which he used to slide down the leading edge to push the weed off. This worked much better, and since we didn't see anyone else using anything like it, we kept the stick hidden inside the boat's double bottom.

Rodney and I made a really good team. He took responsibility for the boat, making sure that nothing broke, while I looked after the sails and talked to the sailmakers. I have always been fascinated by sails and rig tuning and recorded our choice of sails and rig settings for every race during the 1968 season. The shrouds on *Superdocious* were controlled by two 8:1 kicker winch drums set under the side decks, which had swaged loops set at 2in (5cm) intervals within the control wires. The genoa halyard was tensioned with a muscle box under the foredeck and the control line was also calibrated. I recorded all these settings for each sail we used, along with wind speed, sea state (smooth or choppy) and race result. The game plan was to build up a practical database (without a computer!) so we could reproduce the right settings for any sail combination. Just as important, we knew with great accuracy which sails to use in every set of conditions. Nowadays, it would be on an Excel spreadsheet on an iPad, but back then it was just pen and paper.

We tested sails from various lofts and if we won two or three races with a particular genoa or mainsail, Rodney would order an exact replica made from the same batch of sailcloth, which was then stored away together with a sheet of rig settings. We took 32 sails to Acapulco, together with three centreboards, all developed for light, medium and heavy conditions, and from my little blue diary we knew exactly which to use and its optimum setting for every condition. The sails were stored in pairs, the sail that had proven to be a race-winner, with its identical twin, almost unused, but possibly a fraction faster by being brand new.

After spending four weeks getting acclimatised and training every day, I think we measured only eight or nine sails for the week of the Olympics, because the wind was almost the same every day, in the 5–10mph (8–16kph) range, so we only needed to measure light wind sails, with a couple of 10–15mph (8–16kph) sails just in case. The whole game boiled down to getting enough power from the sails to get the crew out on the trapeze, and then the boat was a rocketship.

Rodney and I had our dissenters within the British FD fleet, mainly for not training or sharing things with them. This bugged Keith Musto and John Oakeley in particular, who saw us as being aloof and selfish. Rodney and I tended to gravitate towards people with technical backgrounds, and for every dissenter at home, we had four or five top European crews who would train and tune up with us and posed no threat to our Olympic selection. We became firm friends with men like West German champion Ulli Libor, the Green brothers from Canada and top French sailors such as Alain Draeger, sailmaker Bertrand Chéret, and Bruno Troublé, who went on to skipper two French America's Cup challengers. They were boatbuilders, sailmakers and engineers, were happy to give us a leg up, and we socialised together a lot. Rodney could be loud and aggressive in the boat, but ashore with friends he wasn't hostile, aggressive or unfriendly. People often asked, "How do you deal with his yelling and shouting?" I was young, learning an enormous amount about sailing and didn't care what he called me so long as we were winning races. That was what made me happy. I thought it was just a way of letting off steam, and we never came ashore with any arguments or bad feelings, just satisfaction in winning the race.

I did a lot of the tactics from out on the wire because Rodney couldn't always see clearly whether we were going to cross ahead of other boats or not. He was never a good communicator, and rarely thought to give a warning call: "Ready About ... Lee Ho." Instead, I learned to anticipate his actions. "There's a shift" would invariably mean "Tack" and I would be in off the wire the moment he put the helm down.

Rodney has never shown much interest in the logistics of life. Going to the supermarket to buy energy foods such as fruit and juices was never a priority and he always relies on others to do this for him. He really thrived within his home environment and his mum made sure that everything ran smoothly. She would feed us well and made sure we had clean shirts and shorts every day. That left him to focus almost entirely on whatever made the boat go fast.'

All change

Iain's departure left me to plan a new FD campaign for the 1972 Olympics in a new boat and with a new crew, and also to think carefully about my career in the Navy. I had returned to active duty at the end of 1968, joining the submarine HMS *Grampus* as 3rd Lieutenant. Conveniently, *Grampus* was based at HMS *Dolphin* in Portsmouth.

By now, I realised that if I were to focus on a second Olympic campaign, I would have to leave the Navy. I duly submitted my resignation. The issue for me, as it was for the Admiralty too, was timing. My submarine training had been very costly, and there were some within the Navy who wanted to see some return for this investment in the form of active service, whereas others within higher command could see the PR benefit to the service of having me winning European and World titles. In the end, a compromise was struck and I was transferred to ATURM, the Royal Marine training base close to my home in Poole where I served out my time in the unique position of Submarine Liaison Officer.

I had not thought about timing when I handed in my resignation, and when someone calculated that I would have served nine-and-a-half years, the Navy very kindly extended my commission for a further six months so that I was eligible for a £2,000 retirement gratuity. That was very generous and the money allowed me to devote all my energies to winning gold at the 1972 Olympics.

I had been testing out several crews, including Nicholas Davies, a medical student from Lymington who was working at a London hospital. He was a good sailor and we began well, winning the 1970 FD European Championship in Arenys de Mar, Spain, but he was then forced to give up because his hands were getting cut to shreds. I wouldn't allow him to wear gloves because of the loss of sensitivity and the fumbling this leads to when handling sheets and the spinnaker pole. Hands normally harden when working with ropes, but his remained soft because of the bacterial creams he had to rub into them while at work. Nick tried wearing fingerless gloves but still returned to work on Monday mornings looking as if he had spent the weekend working in an abattoir. I guess his patients were put off seeing his hands covered in plasters because his skin never got a chance to heal properly.

I then teamed up with Julian Brooke-Houghton, a very experienced crew who had already won the Fireball World Championship with Peter Bateman. Still racing *Superdocious* at that time, we just managed to win the World Championship in La Rochelle the following year, but there were problems developing. Julian had a bad back, aggravated by wearing the heavyweight jacket filled with water bottles that was necessary in strong breezes. I also felt he lacked the same level of commitment that Iain had given to my previous campaign and in 1971 the partnership broke down due to what divorce lawyers would call 'irreconcilable differences'.

I was back to looking for a new crew, and my flatmate David Robinson, who had just been appointed to the new role of Olympic coach by the Royal Yachting Association, introduced me to his former Merlin Rocket crewman, Chris Davies. He was already racing an FD with Hamble-based boatbuilder/designer Hugh Welbourn, but their campaign had run out of money. My brother John also knew him from their team-racing days at university, and Chris joined me in September 1971 for a four-day training session with the top French FD sailors at Quiberon. He was extremely keen and our winning relationship developed from there on.

In the meantime, I had ordered a new boat from Bob Hoare. She was one of the first to be pulled off a new mould that Bob had produced to take advantage of an advanced vacuum-moulding technique perfected by Gougeon Brothers in Michigan, USA, where they built lightweight iceboats to race on the Great Lakes during the winter months. It was a much faster building process, which was important for Bob because, since our win in Acapulco, everyone it seemed wanted to buy a copy of *Superdocious*. The West System epoxy glue used to coat the wood veneers promised a lighter, stronger construction and Bob had built a new mould strong enough to take the pressure that the vacuum-bagging curing process placed on it. When the hull and deck were complete, Chris and I devoted many hours to fairing the bottom and producing a perfect finish. It was a lot of effort but we both had high hopes that she would be a big improvement on the now ageing and heavy *Superdocious*.

Trials and tribulations with *Superdoso*

I named her *Supercalifragilisticexpialidoso*, the Spanish spelling of the Mary Poppins song, in deference to Elsa Polin, a girlfriend I had met at the Yacht Club in Acapulco who gave me a Mexican lucky charm the day we were disqualified from the first race. I'm not normally superstitious, but after Iain and I had won our gold medals, I wore this gold charm continuously until I lost it in the showers during the 1986 French multihull championship in La Trinité-sur-Mer, France. That loss somehow coincided with a dive in my competitive sailing career, and for a time I had to be content with second-best placings until I forced myself to dispense with superstition.

The new boat, dubbed *Superdoso*, was unlucky from the start. During our first regatta at Palamós, Spain, Ulli Libor T-boned us, his bows punching a hole right through our port quarter, causing considerable damage. I had the new boat repaired in Spain, then caught a ferry to the next regatta in Genoa, where I had been invited to compete on an expenses-paid basis – funded, I found out later, by the Italian Sailing Federation led by Beppe Croce, who was also president of the International Yacht Racing Union, the governing body of the sport. Had I known beforehand, I would have had second thoughts, because the Italian Yachting Federation under Croce had set me up for a 'sting' the last time I had competed in Italy.

The Italian incident

Shortly after our Olympic success in Mexico, I received an expenses-paid invitation to compete in an FD regatta at Forte dei Marmi, Italy. After the prize-giving, the club secretary presented me with a large envelope stuffed with lire. I counted out the exact amount to cover all the travelling receipts and gave the money that remained back to the secretary. I was being straight, taking payment only for items allowed by the rules governing amateur status at the time, and could not understand his reluctance to take back the large amount of cash that I could not account for. Was I naive?

The first I knew that I had been stitched up was in November that year when Vernon Stratton called me from the IYRU Conference in London saying: 'Rodney, we have a problem.' Beppe Croce had stood up at the conference and announced that he had proof that I had breached my amateur status by accepting a large cash expenses payment and should be barred from competing in any further Olympics. It came as a huge shock and it was only Vernon's quick thinking that saved the day. We learned that the secretary had pocketed the rest of the cash for his club, thinking perhaps it would not be missed, and not realising the wider part he was playing in this sting. Fortunately, I was not sailing a single-handed dinghy and had my crewman as a witness. I certainly needed one!

In Genoa, I found myself under the influence of Beppe Croce again, but at the time the biggest problem appeared to be a lack of wind. A high-pressure system sat resolutely over the whole Liguria region and I questioned whether we were going to get any racing in at all. I did not want Chris Davies flying out from London on a wasted journey and decided to take up the offer of French 505 sailor François Richard to stand in for him. The issue was that Chris had the measurement certificate for the new boat, and with fax machines still an expensive novelty at that time, this caused a problem with the organisers. The club secretary readily agreed for a copy of the certificate to be sent later, but when we finally completed two races, Croce, whose influence extended to being commodore of the Genoa club, saw that we were not fast and instructed the club secretary to send me home – without paying any travel expenses. I was incensed, but there is very little you can do to counter Italian obstinacy and, worst of all, their pride.

Back in Poole, I began to have serious doubts about the new boat and decided to two-boat test it against *Superdocious*. The old boat just shot ahead and after switching sails, centreboards and other variables it was clear to me and Richard Roscoe, my long-term sparring partner in the old boat, that there was something fundamentally wrong. Chris added that from his view out on the wire the motion of the two boats over the waves was completely different. Compared with *Superdocious*, the new boat didn't lift up and plane nearly as easily.

Bob Hoare remained unconvinced, assuring me that his new creation was exactly the same shape as the old boat. I had to organise a second two-boat test to convince him otherwise. What to do? The Olympic trials were less than two months away and he had a full order book for his new West System epoxy boats. As we discussed the options, Bob suddenly mentioned that he still had the old mould from which *Shadow* and *Superdocious* had been taken, hidden out of sight in his back garden. He felt there was just time to build another boat, and pressed his loyal lads to cold-mould it between the rain showers in the open behind his heated shed where all the second generation of boats were being built. It was ironic really to watch numerous foreign Olympic competitors pick up their new hi-tech boats with no idea that they would never be as fast as Bob Hoare's original model.

The deformities within my hull developed during the vacuum-curing process; the position of the large crude heaters that Bob set around the mould to cook the epoxy-coated veneers did not provide a uniform heat and led to the mould distorting. This wasn't obvious to the eye, but careful measurement later showed one side to have a different curvature to the other and, worse, that the keel line was distorted – faults that made a considerable difference to boat speed.

During the moulding and finishing of this third boat, I got Bob's men to replicate the signs of repair made to the second boat, and swore everyone to secrecy. Fortunately, Bob had never got round to stamping the build number on the slow boat, so the new hull took on the certification and sail number (K263) from the boat it was replacing. That way, no one would know that I had a new boat. The reject was given a later hull number and a fresh coat of paint, and Bob sold it as 'slightly used' at a bargain price to a Mexican customer who used it for club racing on a beautiful lake outside Guadalajara.

My 'ghost boat', as she became known, was built in quite a rush – three weeks from start to finish, with several 24-hour sessions needed to have her ready for Kiel pre-Olympic Week, our final regatta before the final British selection trials at Weymouth.

Chris and I drove straight to Kiel and arrived on the Friday, leaving precious little time to prepare before racing got under way the following day. She was launched for the first time late in the day and we took her for a test sail. Harold Cudmore, who was to qualify for Ireland at the Olympics, was also out sailing and suggested that we hook up for a quick practice session. That really suited me because we had no idea at this stage how fast the ghost boat might be. We outsailed the Irish FD on every point of sail and when Harold returned to shore, our rivals crowded round him to find out how the trial had gone. 'I might just as well burn my boat,' he answered with typical Irish wit.

The 100-strong FD fleet represented a 'who's who' of dinghy racing talent, with all our top Olympic rivals competing. The new

Superdoso dominated the week, winning all seven races. The fact that we were disqualified from one fluky race for being over the line at the start after finishing an hour ahead of our nearest rival didn't matter a jot. We had delivered a crushing psychological blow by showing a clear speed advantage over our Olympic rivals. All that time and effort to build a new boat had been well invested and I could not have been happier.

We returned to England full of expectation for the impending UK Olympic trials at Weymouth. A new rule restricting the use of equipment and spars had been imposed for this regatta that banned crews from making any changes once the regatta had begun, unless to replace a breakage. The weather had been so benign and the forecast predicted only light or moderate winds for much of the week ahead, so I selected the stiffer Alspar mast rather than the Elvstrøm spar, which was better in a blow. It was a near-fatal mistake.

The first race coincided with a run of unexpected low-pressure systems that presented us with strong south-westerlies and Chris and I found ourselves at a serious disadvantage. Being one of the lightest crews in the fleet, we were no match upwind against the heavier crews, and though our lighter weight helped downwind, we found ourselves outclassed in what for many were survival conditions.

Keith Musto, the 1964 silver medallist, was sailing with Peter Sweetman, a bear of a man when compared with Chris's 13 stone (82.5kg), and they were in very good form, and while we struggled to overcome a series of mishaps, they gained a considerable points advantage and looked set to win selection to the Games. As we returned to the beach after the first race, a film crew hooked up with us to shoot *Superdoso* surfing down the waves. The driver of their RIB failed to anticipate our acceleration; we became caught up in their steep wake, tripped over it and capsized. This was not deliberate, but that didn't stop everyone thinking it was. Something very similar had happened to Paul Elvstrøm just prior to 1952 Olympics in Helsinki: he was not happy with the wooden mast he had been issued for his Finn dinghy, and it broke in mysterious circumstances during a training session, which meant that the future gold medallist had been allowed to replace it.

While we were righting *Superdoso*, the spreader bracket parted from the mast. Ironically. Suspicion immediately fell on me. Was the damage deliberate? Was it repairable? Chris and I drove back to spend the night at my home in Poole, leaving Vernon Stratton to argue our case before the jury. The spreader bracket could not be repaired or replaced in time for the following day's race because it was a tailor-made fitting and the welding had broken. Vernon contended that a replacement mast was the only solution. The jury agreed, and on our return to Weymouth the following morning we were given permission to swap masts amid howls of indignation from our rivals.

The strong winds continued and seconds before the next race, the flexible wire round a shroud winch suddenly snapped. I luffed hard into wind and fortunately saved the mast from breaking, but the damage left us with no alternative but to retire. Back on the beach, I realised that we had sprung the Elvstrøm mast, and though we attempted to straighten it, I knew that the bend characteristics would now vary from one tack to the other, and applied for another replacement. Bruised by accusations of favouritism after the decision the previous day, the jury felt pressured to refuse this second request, saying that they would reserve judgement until they had monitored our performance in the races that followed.

Someone exacerbated what was already a tense situation by sticking a card up on the Royal Dorset YC noticeboard reading:

'FOR SALE
1 almost new Alspar FD mast with footprints only as far as the spreaders.'

Journalist Bob Fisher was thought to have been the likely culprit, but asked about this recently, he told me in the clearest terms: 'I denied it then … I and deny it now 40 years later!' The finger of guilt now points to the late Doug Bishop, another prankster in the class. Whatever the case, this and the supposed injustice of allowing us to replace our mast served to unsettle Keith and Peter just enough to give us a chance of winning through.

Our next result was mediocre to say the least, which convinced the jury to allow us to make a second change. By now, Musto and

Sweetman had a convincing lead, but there was still a chance for us to win the trials. Then Lady Luck came close to deserting us again. Close to the finish of the fourth race, while challenging Johnson Wooderson and Paul Davies for the lead, I attempted to bear away and blast through their lee and cross the line, only to be stopped in our tracks by a sudden cracking noise. To my horror, I found that the centreboard had split in two. We just managed to sideslip across the far end of the line and retain our second place, and I began to wonder what else was likely to befall us.

Our backs were now against the wall, and on the final day, with two races scheduled, Musto and Sweetman had only to finish second in one of them to win the Olympic selection. We went afloat pretty disillusioned. Chris and I discussed whether to sit on Keith at the start and, once he was buried in the fleet, rely on *Superdoso*'s speed advantage in the lighter conditions to carry us through to the front. But there were others in the fleet who were very competitive, too, and in the end we relied simply on our boat speed and left fate to deal with the rest. We won both races by more than two minutes, followed by Wooderson and Davies who, by finally getting their act together, pushed Musto and Sweetman down to third. We won selection by the skin of our teeth and Musto, with Paul Davies as crewman, came to Kiel as our tune-up crew and reserve skipper and crew and played a vital role in supporting my attempt to win a second successive gold medal.

We again had weather guru David Houghton from the National Weather Centre with us to forecast with great accuracy what we could expect in terms of wind strength and patterns, and Vernon drew on the lessons learned from Acapulco four years before to bring us all to peak at these Games. However, team preparations were disrupted by a dispute over coaching strategy between Stratton, as manager, and team coach David Robinson. This led to Vernon barring David from coming to Kiel with the team. The media had a field day, with Jack Knights stirring things up most in his column in *Yachts & Yachting* magazine, and some crews took delight in needling us and our obvious discomfort over this spat.

David did get to Kiel, but as personal assistant to Owen Aisher, then chairman of the RYA. This gave the perfect opportunity for

Alan Warren and David Hunt, racing in the Tempest keelboat class, to wind Stratton up. When Vernon knocked on their bedroom door early each morning to get them to join the team training run, the pair gave a succession of weak explanations as to why they were too tired for any such exercise. Then, as soon as Stratton had left the hotel, they rushed to run up and down stairs just long enough to be back in bed feigning sleep when the team manager returned.

The Tempest course was set furthest out in the Baltic and crews had to set out early each day to reach the area in time for their start. Warren and Hunt spent this time idly thinking about what Vernon might not have in his RIB when he did the rounds to check that everyone was fully prepared. One time they asked for a 32-part purchase for their kicking strap, whereupon Stratton rushed back to get the necessary blocks, only to return for them to say 'Oh, thanks Vernon, but David sorted us out.'

Before that year's Games, the IOC had reinforced the rules governing the amateur status of athletes by forbidding advertisers from naming Olympic competitors in their advertisements. I had written to all my suppliers telling them to delete all mention of my name from future advertising, but this had not reached Helmsman Paint's American agent, who thought the run-up to the 1972 Olympics was the perfect time to run an advert endorsing my choice of Graphspeed bottom paint for *Superdocious* during the 1968 Games and naming me.

The offending endorsement appeared in the following full-page advertisement in one of the American sailing magazines:

'Graphspeed proved to win

Britain's gold medal winners chose the finest racing bottom finish in the world.

Rodney Pattisson and Iain MacDonald-Smith chose the proven advantage of Graphspeed for *Superdocious.*'

The first I knew of this was when the Americans protested my amateur status on the eve of the Olympic regatta. It was a deliberate attempt to affect our morale and Vernon Stratton had to work long and hard to defend my position. Fortunately, I had copies of my correspondence with Helmsman Paint to prove the matter and Vernon dealt with it brilliantly. This challenge probably helped him to refocus his energies on an issue much more important than the 'Robinson Affair', and in dealing with it so well, he saved me from having to fly down to Munich and face an IOC hearing, which would have been a severe distraction. Of course, the American protest was timed to cause maximum disruption and served as a reminder once more that you have no friends when it comes to Olympic competition.

During the regatta we were blessed with light to medium winds throughout the week and won our Olympic crown with a race to spare. Fortunately, the terrible Palestinian terrorist massacre of 11 Israeli team members in the Olympic village at Munich had no direct affect on us, for we won our gold medals that same day, 5 September, and were given the awful news only after coming ashore. The atrocity played out for 20 hours before ending with a botched rescue at a military airport outside Munich, and wiped out any wish to celebrate our success. Thankfully, we had won with a race to spare and did not have to sail on the final day, having chalked up a scoreline of 11th, 3rd, 1st, 1st, 1st, 1st and finished with 12 points in all.

Alan Warren and David Hunt had to be content with silver medals after a wind shift during the final beat of their deciding race robbed them of first place and lifted the Ukrainian Valentyn Mankin up from ninth to take the gold for the USSR. It was a cruel blow, but the pair took it all very philosophically, the sailing team returning home with a clutch of gold and silver medals between us.

Winning a second gold was testament to the single-minded approach and sacrifices that all successful Olympians have to make. So, after all the plaudits, I was astounded to find that Chris Davies was the sole British gold medallist to have been omitted from the New Year honours list; every other British Olympic winner in single and team disciplines was awarded an MBE, following a precedent set by Harold Wilson after the 1968 Games when I and Iain McDonald-Smith had the honour of receiving ours. Had Chris simply been forgotten, or was there something more sinister? My questions were met by a wall of silence and led to a three-decade-long battle to have this slight redressed.

The answer was finally revealed when government Cabinet papers were released. The issue related to an unexpected visit to the

Kiel Olympic regatta centre by Prime Minister Edward Heath to congratulate Chris and me. I was not there, and Chris, who, like me, had abstained from alcohol for more than a year, was having a quiet celebration with his then fiancée and friends. It transpired that Heath had been offended by some over-familiar remarks that Chris had made. The Cabinet papers revealed a note, probably written by one of Heath's aides, stating: 'This man is not to be honoured in any way.'

Chris finally got his MBE in 2001, 29 years after this incident, and only after a sustained campaign supported by sailors, Olympic champions, the press and social media (see Chapter 5).

Chris Davies on Rodney

'It was David Robinson who first introduced me to Rodney. I got a call at short notice asking if I would crew for him at a training regatta in Quiberon, France. My instructions were to meet at the ferry terminal, walk down the line of cars until I found a Morgan with a Flying Dutchman in tow, and climb in. That was our first meeting. Rodney never did confirm that he wanted me to stay with him for the rest of the campaign, but I got another call to sail with him the following weekend and assumed that he did.

I had no long-term ambition to go to the Olympics but I was fanatically keen on dinghy racing and had been racing with and against many of Britain's elite sailors at national championship level. But Rodney proved a cut above all these, and so focused. Suddenly, I found myself sailing with someone even keener than I, and thought…WOW! All I have to do is rise to his standard and I had no problem with trying my hardest to achieve that. We were never bosom buddies, and Rodney was not easy to live with, but I only had to do this for a year. I was keen to learn and up for anything he wanted me to do, and I happily gave everything to the campaign.

I was Rodney's third real crew and came into a well-developed system. He had pared everything down to just the things that mattered. It was all very slick with nothing superfluous. Rodney had his methods and fetishes, but his way of preparing for a championship was well-proven and better than most.

Rodney is the steadiest helmsman I have ever sailed with; his boat handling is superb and he sailed so smoothly, never allowing the boat to heel, that I was never caught out on the wire unexpectedly. He did very little adjusting during a race, though he could reposition the centreboard under load from either side deck, which no one else could do at the time.

Rodney introduced me to two-boat tuning. Done the Pattisson way, it is amazing. We had two near-identical boats in K163 and K263 and everything was interchangeable. We could spend 10–12 hours a day testing genoas in light, medium and strong winds, swapping the sail from one boat to the other to double-check results. Halyard settings and sheet positions for each sail were logged for each wind strength, which meant that we always had a good starting point for every sail, and were invariably fast straight out of the blocks. At regattas, we would set the boat up according to these figures and Rodney would make only minor intuitive adjustments before a start and generally not touch anything again unless conditions changed considerably during the race.

He always preferred to have a competent helmsman on the wire, one who could feed him detailed information about wind patterns, and about the performance and position of other boats, and how they were going through the waves. That allowed him to concentrate on boat speed.

One of my jobs was to call out our compass headings, but I had no influence on Rodney's tactical calls. He was totally focused on speed and if I thought it very important to tack I would have to exaggerate the change in bearing.

He seldom seemed to look backwards and the only time he would frighten the life out of me was on the few occasions we made a second-rank start. I knew he would throw in a blind tack within seconds of a start and had to be ready. We would then scream across the fleet on port tack, reaching down at ridiculous speeds to pass inches behind other boats. The reason we didn't hit anyone was purely down to Rodney's extraordinary boat handling, and we would invariably emerge on the right-hand side of the course having turned a bad start into a brilliant one.

I was never worried if he got cross. The angrier he became the better his performance and he never let any situation get the better of him. Pressure was never higher than during the 1972 Olympic trials, a level of tension that I had never experienced before, but Rodney took it all in his stride. Weighing 13 stone (82.6kg), I was light by FD crew standards and we were one of the lightest crews in the fleet. That meant we were never going to compete on level terms upwind against the heavyweights when the breeze was strong, whatever mast we had. During those Olympic trials, Rodney never lost sight of the big picture and was always ready to take every advantage the moment conditions turned in our favour.

Rodney never really mixed with other crews, and at Weymouth he preferred to drive the 30 miles (48km) back home to Poole each night. Home was a wonderful refuge, and I was treated as part of the family.

At the Olympics everyone thought Rodney would win and I didn't want to be the one to lose him his medal. Once we had won, my job was done and the pressure was off. Rodney was the double gold medal winner and the person the media wanted to talk to. I had been teetotal for 12 months and had just downed two stiff drinks to celebrate when Ted Heath came into the room to congratulate us and I greeted him rather inappropriately.

I was never too concerned about getting an honour, but what really pleased me was that Rodney thought I should get one and fought resolutely for three decades to get me an MBE. That meant much more than the medal itself.'

1976 Olympic Campaign

The 1976 Olympic regatta was held in Kingston, Ontario where the St Lawrence River flows out of Lake Ontario. After Kiel, I stepped back from the Olympic circus for a period to develop a business importing Roga 470 dinghies from Spain. It took a couple of years to get back into serious sailing in an FD, and I teamed up with Mike Brooke – a tall, supremely fit Royal Marine officer who had previously campaigned a Tempest with Jack Knights during the build-up to the 1972 Games. He was fanatically keen and we went on to win the 1975 FD European Championship in Travemünde, Germany. It was time to develop a new boat, and I worked with Bob Hoare to experiment with changes in rocker and transom profile in an effort to improve on the old *Superdocious* shape. A flatter rocker increases speed downwind and we experimented with this in a boat built for a Canadian friend who had crewed for me at Forte dei Marmi. Mike and I raced this boat at the 1975 World Championship in Buffalo, Ohio. The experiment failed, for the trade-off between speed gains off the wind compared with what we lost upwind were too great and sadly we did not retain the most magnificent of trophies, a full-sized silver sombrero presented by the Mexicans.

It was back to the drawing board in more ways than one, for with less than a year to the Olympics, I not only needed a new boat but also sensed that my relationship with Mike was unlikely to last the whole distance. The boat was the easier of the two to resolve. Bob Hoare produced another of his tried-and-tested standard hulls for me using the West epoxy system and a reshaped mould almost identical to that used for *Superdocious.*

By early 1976, I had come to the conclusion that Mike and I did not have the right synergy to win a third gold medal. I have always owned my boats, never partnering with crews as Oakeley and Hunt had done, because any break-up invariably leaves a stalled campaign. Instead, I 'employed' my crews so that I could say goodbye to them for whatever reason. Mike did not take well to our parting and the relationship soured, but I am pleased to see that three decades on he continues to have a passion for sailing. In 2008, he completed a solo round-Britain circumnavigation in his 19ft Cape Cutter, *Theo's Future*, raising some £54,000 for the Moorfields Eye Hospital and the UCL Institute of Ophthalmology, to develop gene therapy for children with Leber congenital amaurosis (LCA).

Four months before the Montreal Olympics I still needed someone I knew and trusted, someone totally capable, so I offered an olive branch to Julian Brooke-Houghton. He was the most naturally talented crew I have ever sailed with, and with the evil weight jackets that had led to our parting after winning the 1976 World Championship now banned, I understood he had overcome his back problems for good. It was not an easy decision for either of us: he viewed my single-minded approach to winning as fanaticism, and I had not liked the party animal within him. Nevertheless, we decided to put these issues aside because of the strong prospect we had of winning gold medals together.

The new boat (K300) arrived in the final year and carried another variation on *Supercalifragilisticxpialidoso* with an 'x' substituting the middle 'e'. The media called her *Superdoso* just the same. Unlike 1968 and 1972, this was a very last-minute campaign, relying on past developments and experience, and we sailed through the selection trials relatively easily, this time without any breakages!

The Robinson Affair that had blown up at Kiel tested relations between Vernon Stratton and the RYA's Olympic Committee to breaking point and Robin Aisher, who had won a bronze medal at Acapulco, was appointed British Team Manager instead. Thankfully, we still had David Houghton as our weather guru, and his microanalysis of the conditions at Kingston proved invaluable. After two races, everything seemed to be going to plan, with us heading the leader board with a first and second. But then the wheels fell off in a big way. Having banned weight jackets, the FD Class had adopted new rules to control crew clothing allowance in an effort to level the playing field, and Julian and I had a major falling out over his carelessness. Our relationship had already cooled after a previous clash during pre-race training. We had been two-boat testing a series of new sails against Keith Musto and Paul Davies, and had one more to check out when Julian insisted on returning to shore because he had a 'date'. I couldn't believe it. What were we here for – to win medals or socialise? We did go back ashore without testing the sail, but he remained so angry, I learned later, that he threatened to quit before the event started. It was only Keith Musto's fatherly intervention that persuaded him to stay, saying that he was representing not only Britain but the British FD fleet and that he would be letting down both if he departed at this stage. It was a measure of Julian's stoicism that he did stay and put everything into winning a medal.

Before the start to race three, Julian had put on a third vest because he said he was getting cold. Once we had finished, we stripped off most of our upper clothing for the sail back to the dock before a jury boat came up to tell us that we had been selected for a spot check on clothing. The crew then escorted us back to base to ensure that nothing was thrown overboard. Looking at our discarded clothing heaped in a pile within the boat, I asked: 'Julian. Are you going to be OK at the weigh-in?' It was only then that he mentioned the extra vest, which would almost certainly make him overweight and get us disqualified. Thankfully, I knew that I was underweight, and because the jury official could not differentiate one piece of clothing in the pile from another, I said testily, 'When we gather up our gear for weighing, that extra vest had best be mine.' We got away with it – just, but I was angry. Julian knew the rules just as well as I. He had not only been careless but totally unprofessional, and it tested our partnership almost to breaking point.

Midway through the week, we were to experience what can only be described as the flukiest race in history. The race organisers knew that with a sunny forecast the early land breeze would soon be opposed by a sea breeze once the land had heated up, leaving a strong prospect of calms. Rather than delay racing until reliable winds filled in, the race committee began on time in the hope that racing would be concluded before the land breeze faded. The three classes on our course – the Dutchmen, the Tempests and the Solings – all got away on time, with ten minutes between starts.

Soon after our start the wind became very fluky, gusting one minute and shifting wildly the next. The coaches watching from their RIBs were as dismayed by the changing conditions as those competing, for the race became a complete lottery. Somehow, Julian and I led around the final leeward mark and were still leading two-thirds up the beat when the breeze finally faded to zero. There is only one thing more frustrating than sitting becalmed within shouting distance of the finish, and that is watching helplessly as the tail-end Charlie pulls through the fleet to win. That is what happened with Hans Fogh, the Danish-born sailmaking protégé of Paul Elvstrøm. He had rounded the leeward mark last, caught the first breath of sea breeze coming up from astern and, hoisting a spinnaker, had sailed around the entire fleet to take the winning gun.

Worse, the leaders of the Tempest and Soling Classes piled in behind him, with only a minute or so separating them – remarkable when you consider they had started 10 and 20 minutes behind us! Most were so disgruntled that the majority within the three fleets decided to protest the race in an effort to have the results annulled. The jury agreed to a hearing, but allowed only three representatives from each class to present their cases.

The chairman of the jury was none other than my friend and enemy Beppe Croce, the Italian President of the IYRU who had tried to discredit my amateur status three years before. He had no wish to have the race rerun, and used his autocratic authority over fellow jury members to rebuff all argument. The racing instructions, for instance, allow for a race to be rerun in the event of a major wind shift during the first beat. Having this happen during the final beat when recovery was impossible is a far worse scenario. Turning to me, Croce discounted this, saying, 'You were just unlucky.' I pointed out that 'luck' was not a word used within the rulebook. The correct word was 'fair', and the rules required a race to be just that. He countered that, saying that the words 'luck' and 'fair' were one and the same in Italian, a stupid response that should have drawn some comment from other members of the International Jury, but they were too weak to stand up to the man. For all the input they provided, they might just as well have not been there at all!

The race was of course allowed to stand because Croce said in his statement that an annulment of the results would have set a precedent. In fact, his decision did quite the opposite, setting a dangerous precedent that would force future juries to disregard wild vagaries in the weather that turned race results upside down. We all regarded it as a very bad day for the sport and fair sailing in the future.

During race four I had witnessed a clear breach of the racing rules against the French Pajot brothers by another crew sailing on the 'give way' port tack. Inexplicably, the French did not wish to protest so I threatened a third-party protest against both boats if the Pajots took no action. Unbeknown to me, the offending crew had already been found guilty of breaking the same port and starboard right-of-way rule the day before and knew that a second disqualification would rule them out of medal contention. Another member of their team came over to see me before the hearing, threatening me if I protested. He gave me a quiet but chilling warning, that if I went ahead and his crew lost, they would make sure that I didn't win a medal either. With typical obstinacy, I refused to be blackmailed, and the ensuing protest, not by me but by the Pajot brothers in the end, led to the offending crew's disqualification.

The following day, the guilty crew found themselves dead ahead of us at the start of the two long reaching legs. I realised their intent to luff each time I tried to pass, so although we had the faster boat my only safe option was to follow in their wake, not daring to overtake in case of losing a valuable place in the fleet.

The next day it was even worse. Ahead of us at the leeward mark for the final beat to the finish, they were there, sails flapping, and covered us tack-for-tack to the finish. We tried everything to break their cover, even several dummy tacks, but to no avail. I felt like protesting, but what was the point? They might have been disqualified for unsportsmanlike behaviour but it would have been our word against theirs. And besides, whatever the jury decided, our poor finishing position would remain. The possibility of winning gold was now gone and the German Deisch brothers were now leading on points by a considerable margin. We desperately needed a good final result if we were to secure a medal at all. So I wrote a personal letter to the jury, in the hope that they might just do something; after all, unsportsmanlike behaviour is a serious sin in sport. Beppe Croce, chairman of the jury, did acknowledge my letter, and felt slightly sorry for us, but explained that he could do nothing about it.

Fortunately the final race went well for us. It was a reasonable result with no interference, the offending crew, for whatever reason, keeping well clear. I suspect the jury had an unofficial word with their team manager. Rumours too by that time were circulating around the dinghy park, as we had many good friends among our foreign competitors. They knew something was up, noticing that our results had become so poor, and might have learned why. They too may have had words with the culprits. Looking back, I sometimes think that Vernon Stratton, our former team manager, might have handled things better.

Many years later I mentioned the matter to my great New Zealand FD rivals, Jock Bilger and Murray Ross, who had competed in the same three Olympic Games as me, and were always strong competition. Murray made the following statement:

'During the sixth race, just after rounding the leeward mark for the final beat, I witnessed another competitor sitting with sails loosely sheeted, partly flapping. I thought they must have had a breakage, but when Rodney and Julian rounded the leeward mark, the competitor sheeted their sails on and proceeded to put cover on the GB boat, tacking continuously on top of them in classic match racing moves. What was very strange to me was their tactics were not only causing the GB boat to lose many places but also themselves. It was the most unusual behaviour I have seen in the twelve years that I have sailed with Jock Bilger in FD regattas.'

Even a win in that last race would not have been enough to dislodge the German Diesch brothers from gold, but a good place was sufficient to lift us up to silver, just ahead of the Brazilians. But this issue soured the pleasure of winning my third Olympic medal. I would have gladly accepted the silver if we had been beaten fair and square, but we were not. The incident really marked the end of my Olympic days, for had I won gold, the incentive would have been there to try to emulate the great Paul Elvstrøm's record of four successive Olympic gold medals.

Julian Brooke-Houghton on Rodney

'Rodney has been dedicated to sailing for every waking moment, winning every race that is put in front of him. He is meticulous to the point of distraction, very, very talented and channels his obsession into making small incremental gains, just as Britain's cycling team has developed domination within their sport in more recent times.

I was fortunate to start my FD sailing with John Truett, who worked extremely hard in a very methodical fashion before going on to build up a long-standing and successful partnership with Peter Bateman in Fireballs and FDs. He and I sailed together with a lot of commitment and harmony without stress or worry, a flow that I never had with Rodney.

A major part of the crew's job is to get the best out of the helmsman, and if for instance that means putting up with their shouting, that's what you do. Rodney always treated his crews as if they were the least reliable part of the boat and his shouting was really an expression of his energy, a valve that he needed to open. He wasn't very good at crewing himself, so I simply gave the impression of doing what he thought was right while quietly doing what I knew to be better.

He was very shy, reluctant to join in socially and to speak to the press. We sailed together in the FD World Championship at La Rochelle in 1971, but after Kiel Week that year I was getting so wound up that I felt I couldn't continue sailing with him. So it was a surprise to me when in the run-up to the 1976 Olympics he asked me to sail with him again. My immediate response was, "Well, that isn't going to

work is it?" But Rodney was persistent and we found a way to
work together again.

Rodney has often been energised by adversity, as in
earlier Olympics and trials. Reflecting on our silver medal
performance in Kingston, Peter Bateman, by then a member
of the British coaching squad, said to me, "You know what you
should have done – fallen off the trapeze or done something
equally crass in that first race. Rodney would have been
almost unbearable for the rest of the week but much faster as
a result.'"

1980 Olympic campaign

In preparation for the next Games, I ordered a new fibre-reinforced
plastic FD from the Italian manufacturer Bianchi & Cecchi, the
moulding of which was very similar to the Hoare shape. I also
accepted sponsorship for the first time, kindly supplied by Otis Lifts,
and teamed up with Andrew Cooper, a tall, very fit submariner in
the Royal Navy.

Off the water, the build-up to the 1980 Olympics was being
frustrated by the Russian invasion of Afghanistan and the mixing
of politics and sport. The Russians had just invaded Afghanistan,
which caused a political storm across Europe and would eventually
lead to a partial boycott of the Moscow Olympics and the Olympic
regatta in Tallinn, Estonia. We were racing at the ski-yachting
regatta in Cannes with the American Olympic team when President
Carter announced that the USA was to boycott the Moscow Games
in protest over the invasion.

I felt very strongly about the invasion and decided to start a
petition among sailors competing at Cannes to show the Russian
crews that the rest of the world did not condone such aggressive
behaviour.

I typed out a strongly worded petition for all to sign. The Russian
sailors read it and were shocked. They knew nothing of the invasion
or the attitude of the western world towards it. A few crews from
behind the Iron Curtain even signed the petition, along with many

from Poland and Czechoslovakia. Not everyone was so forward. I remember the Afghan coach coming up to me in an agitated state demanding the removal of his team's signatories, saying that I needed to understand that he had the Russian army in residence and that if this became known there would be repercussions.

The French authorities also took a different view. Unbeknown to us, the French Sailing Federation had developed a cosy relationship with its opposite number in Russia to provide reciprocal hospitality for teams whenever they were competing in each other's country; French officials therefore did their best to quell our small protest.

I was not a popular figure, so when it came to competing in the giant slalom skiing section of this event in the Esterel Mountains above Cannes, a ski discipline that I am not very good at, the French organisers were awkwardly surprised when I seemingly flew down the slope straight to the top of the leader board. Surprise turned to anger when the helmet came off to reveal the smiling face and glowing locks of Jane Oundjon, a much better skier than me, who had quietly taken my place in line to save my blushes, bruises and perhaps a broken limb or two. Most laughed at this harmless jape, but not the French, who disqualified me from the competition.

By the time of the pre-Olympic regatta in Hyères, where some crews followed my lead in displaying a black flag on the leech of our mainsails to signal our disgust at the invasion, arguments back home had become just as strong, with Prime Minister Margaret Thatcher announcing that she did not want to see any British teams competing at the Moscow Olympics. Her government left it to the various national sports federations to decide, but since the Royal Yachting Association and the British Equestrian Federation both shared Prince Philip, Duke of Edinburgh, as their president, these were the only sports to fall in line with the government boycott.

This decision taken by the RYA made any Olympic trials superfluous, so after the regatta at Hyères we felt there was no point in continuing our campaign. Also, Andrew was required back on his nuclear submarine for another Polaris patrol. That brought back many past memories. The British trials did take place, but with some of our top hopefuls, me included, missing the event altogether, it was a meaningless regatta. Those who did show up attended in the vain hope that the boycott might be lifted at the last moment. It wasn't of course, and a general lack of wind led to races being cancelled and the series having to be extended, turning a farce into a charade. In the end, Alejandro Abascal and Miguel Noguer from Spain won the FD gold medal at Tallinn against watered-down competition.

Andrew Cooper on Rodney

'Rodney is an enigma. A brilliant sailor, with such a fixation for boat speed and winning, yet at times finding it hard to interact, until you get to know him. Rodney's great strength is his ability to focus exclusively on boat speed, something he can do for hours on end, and when he gets the bit between his teeth – and a bit cross with himself or others – he bubbles like a volcano and is at his very best. The trick was to try and encourage the right balance, at which point he could win by miles.

Like Rodney, I was a Royal Navy submariner, which gave us not only a special bond but a forensic attitude to detail in everything we did. In fact I was introduced to Rodney by fellow naval officer and Olympian Finn/Star sailor David Howlett, the optimum crew requirement being for 12½ stone (79.4kg), 6ft 2in (1.88m) and a helmsman. And this was also in the days of water weight jackets! I learned an enormous amount from Rodney, but my introduction to the front end of a Flying Dutchman was indeed a baptism by fire as I initially lacked some of the acrobatic skills at that level, and didn't have the right kit. He had me wearing a Lycra all-in-one suit to minimise wind resistance and crew weight, but no gloves, so training during the winter months was always a freezing-cold exercise. My introduction to the rubberised Aigle boot was one of the greatest single innovations in staying firmly on the gunnel, even if Rodney wanted me to glue 2in (5cm) platform soles to them to increase the leverage (as had the main German competition)!

At our first regatta in Kiel in 1978 we slept in a two-man tent, the wind blew old boots every day and it proved to be one of the hardest weeks of my life. I was on a very steep learning curve, and surprisingly Rodney had less understanding of the technical requirements needed to be a top-level crew. If I posed a question, I invariably got the response: "Go and ask Julian!" I never did, but I learned the hard way from Rodney – a great privilege I have always cherished.

We had an elite grant from the SportsAid Foundation and lived outside of the RYA's Olympic squad system, which Rodney much preferred. The problem with this was that whenever we did well we got mixed messages from team manager Rod Carr, who for obvious reasons wanted one of his squad to win. That said, I got a lot of moral support from team chairman Vernon Stratton, especially when things got tough – as they did at Weymouth Olympic week in 1979. By the time we got to the Cannes and Hyères pre-Olympic regattas in 1980, we were beginning to work well as a team and were going faster and faster, so the news that the Americans were to boycott the Moscow Olympics and that the whole British team would follow suit was devastating – so much so that we pulled out halfway through the Hyères regatta and went home. Could Rodney have won a third gold medal? Very probably. As it turned out, a partial British boycott was a wasted gesture; the subsequent British trials were a sham and the whole episode cost British Olympic sailing dearly for many years.

I went on to join Rodney and Lawrie Smith as their navigator on board *Victory '83* during that year's America's Cup. Lawrie took charge of the starts and was fantastically fast upwind. Rodney took over on the downwind legs and squeezed every ounce of speed from the boat, often turning a race round before handing the wheel back for Lawrie to do his covering tactics on the final leg. The two made a great partnership. Just a pity that our year coincided with that wonder boat *Australia II*, which beat us in the finals of the Louis Vuitton Challenger trials and went on to win the Cup!'

1984 LA Games

My challenge to represent Britain in the 1984 Games in Los Angeles comprised another last-minute campaign when I made the mistake of relying on hope and experience overcoming my usual preparations. I had been away for a year competing in the America's Cup and although Poole City Council funded a new boat called *Supercalifragilisticexpialidocious of Poole,* I relied too heavily on design and technology improvements to tip the balance. It all sounded great on paper. Ian Howlett, who had designed our America's Cup challenger *Victory '83,* suggested that his considerable experience of testing models in a tank could produce a very fast design, and 'Bungy' Taylor, who had been producing world-class Finn dinghies, offered to mould a hi-tech pre-preg carbon (carbon fibre or glass fabric pre-impregnated with catalysed resin) Flying Dutchman that would not only be lighter, but stiffer than any FD before.

The design was not measurably faster than my Bob Hoare–built boats, but what really upset my plans was the late delivery of the new boat. This was compounded by the fact that the centreboard case had somehow been bonded in askew and further time was lost cutting it out of the boat and rebonding the box in line. Then, the day we launched the boat, shortly before the British trials, the two strips of brushes used as centreboard slot rubbers fell off before we had even sailed the boat, and we lost a further day derigging the boat, turning it upside down and fitting them properly.

Jonathan Clark crewed for me in the trials, but our lack of preparation made it an ordeal simply to compete. We were outclassed by Jo Richards and Peter Allam, who went on to win a bronze medal at the Los Angeles Games.

Just before that Olympic regatta I got an urgent call from the Royal Yachting Association (RYA) because Jo and Peter suddenly found themselves without a tune-up helmsman, rather essential for winning a medal. I jumped at the opportunity, and was able to give the two the benefit of my experience during this final build-up before the regatta. I got a strong sense that Rod Carr, the British team manager, disapproved of the arrangement for I was not part of the British team, and had to leave the Long Beach regatta site on the eve of the Games. I hope my input helped in some way towards Jo and Peter winning their medals, but though they were very grateful to me for flying over at the last minute, there was no acknowledgement from Team GB. Jonathan Janson, who himself was a bronze medallist in the Dragon Class at the 1956 Games, and who served as a vice president of both the RYA and the IYRU, at least extended his thanks at a private dinner on the eve of me leaving Los Angeles. He said how surprised he was that I came at such short notice, and acknowledged that I had worked so hard in support.

Racing through the '80s

I continued racing an FD for a few years and was invited to a regatta in Cadiz, where we finished second to Alejandro Abascal, the 1980 gold medal winner. He got me involved in signing barrels of sherry, which resulted in me spending the evening in a police cell. I had driven him to the vintner's and we had parked the car three floors down in a fume-filled public car park. Alejandro then asked for a last-minute lift to the airport. He was in such a hurry that rather than have us drive back up the spiral to pay at the exit, he found he could lift the bar on a side entrance that led straight out to the street. All would have been well had other sailors, who had made the most of the free sherry, not pointed out to the car park attendant sitting in his booth what they saw us doing on the CCTV screen behind him. The man hit the alarm, and as soon as we reached the road a police car came screaming round the corner. Abascal took off like a scalded cat, leaving me and my crew, David Woolner, to explain ourselves.

At the time, the mood in this region of Spain was very anti-British, with regular barricades and protests on the border with Gibraltar over the UK's determination to keep the Rock within the Union. Catching two criminals in an English-registered car evading a £1 parking fee was manna from heaven, and we were carted off to the police station. Initially, our interrogator pretended that he could not speak English, so I pretended not to speak Spanish, a deadlock that was only broken when David, the innocent passenger, was freed to fetch the yacht club commodore, who provided a bail bond prior to a court hearing in Jerez, 25 miles (40km) away, the following morning.

The commodore took us on a tour of local bars, and somewhere along the line a journalist who had heard about the fracas caught up with us. Whether it was the sherry or the rush of adrenalin following my arrest I don't know, but my usual guard against pressmen was down and I answered his questions rather too candidly.

What stuck in the judge's craw when I faced the bench the following morning was not that we had evaded a £1 parking fee, but that the newspaper reported that I had labelled the parking attendant as 'loco'. I was eventually released with a warning on the understanding that I left £500 in a Spanish bank account to cover any damage to the barrier. I never heard from Alejandro Abascal again, and just hope he caught his plane. It might have been an expensive experience for me had my insurance not covered the bail bond, and for all I know, the £500 is still sitting in that Spanish bank account!

ABOVE AND BELOW: With Iain MacDonald-Smith, sailing *Superdocious* in Poole, UK, *c.*1968. © Eileen Ramsay/PPL

Sailing my Cadet in Swanage Bay, UK, c.1956.
© Rodney Pattisson

Sailing my Firefly in Swanage Bay, UK, c.1959. © Rodney Pattisson

Sailing the Flying Dutchman with Mike, my crew (the future Admiral Boyce), at the Olympic trials held in Poole Bay, UK, 1964. © PPL

With Iain MacDonald-Smith, during the Summer Olympic Games in Acapulco, October 1968. We won the gold medal in the Flying Dutchman class. © Ed Lacey/Popperfoto/Getty Images

Close-up of the multicoloured Superdocious lettering on my Flying Dutchman, now on display at the Maritime Museum in Falmouth, UK. © Jane Southern

With Julian Brooke-Houghton, sailing the Flying Dutchman at the Olympic trials held in Weymouth Bay, UK in 1976. © Alastair Black/PPL

With Iain MacDonald-Smith, racing in heavy weather during the 1970 Flying Dutchman World Championship in Adelaide, Australia, which we won. This was our last regatta together.

Superdocious being towed by my beloved Morgan sports car
outside Parkstone Yacht Club, Poole, UK, *c.*1976.
© Rodney Pattisson

With Francis Joyon (third from right) and his crew at Cowes, UK,
after the Round the Island Race in 2007. © Jane Southern

Sailing my trimaran up to Cowes, UK, 2014.
© Jane Southern

With Iain MacDonald-Smith at the 'queen of British yachting photography' Eileen Ramsay's memorial service in March 2017, with the iconic photo she took of us 49 years earlier in 1968.
© Jane Southern

With Chris Davies, coming ashore having won the gold medal in the penultimate race at the Kiel Olympic Games, 1972. Our commanding lead meant we didn't have to race on the final day.

THREE

Offshore racing

Much of my offshore racing has revolved around the Fastnet and Sydney–Hobart classics, the Admiral's Cup and various Ton Cup events. It is a sad reflection on the sport that apart from the two 600-mile (965km) classic races, most of the others have disappeared. The Admiral's Cup was once revered as the World Championships of offshore racing, and in its heyday it attracted 22 three-boat teams from across the globe. The Ton Cup events were also highly competitive until cheating, rapid obsolescence and the bare discomfort of competing overnight in stripped-out racing machines combined to drive owners away.

The One Ton Cup became one of the holy grails within the sport and many of us made our offshore reputations racing for it. The cup itself stands with the America's Cup as one of the most ornate and coveted pieces of silverware in sailing. Designed in 1897 by Parisian jeweller Robert Linzeler, the 22lb (10kg) solid-silver cup was commissioned by the Cercle de la Voile de Paris and raced for originally in One Ton open day boats selected for the 1900 Paris Olympics. The International Cup event on the River Seine continued to be raced for in Olympic classes until after World War II, when support within the 6m Class dropped away. Jean Peytel, a member of the Cercle de la Voile de Paris, revived the One Ton Cup itself in 1965 in order to encourage international offshore racing.

The first winner was the varnished wooden boat *Diana III* – a classic Sparkman & Stephens design campaigned by Denmark's Hans Albrecht. In 1969 the little-known New Zealand crew led by Chris Bouzaid shipped their S&S-designed *Rainbow II* halfway round the globe to beat the world's best sailors in a closely fought series at Heligoland, a seminal event that not only brought Kiwi sailors to the forefront of international competition for the first time, but also led to a surge of interest in this side of the sport and to the introduction of ¼, ½, ¾ and later Two Ton Cup yachts set at various fixed rating bands to provide open-class racing matched to fixed rating in a variety of boats from 24 to 44ft (7.3 to 13.4m) overall.

Initially, these Cup events drew some wonderful examples of offshore yachts – designs that could be raced competitively, yet provided sufficient comfort below for the owner to take family and friends cruising. Many were produced as series production yachts: the S&S She 36 One Tonner; the 30ft Dufour Arpège (of which 1,500 were built); the Elvstrøm-designed Bes ½ tonners; the Carter 30, 33 and 36 models; and the prototype Contessa 35 *Gumboots* that Jeremy Rogers skippered to victory in the 1974 One Ton Cup – all of which were not only good-looking but comfortable to live aboard, too.

But then offshore racing took a wrong turn when the patients took control of the asylum. The design rules, managed by designers, were tinkered with continually, making boats obsolescent within a year, a move encouraged by builders and sailmakers to force owners to commission new and increasingly extreme boats each season just to remain competitive. Toilets were replaced with buckets; galleys were reduced to a gimballed single-burner camping stove and removable plastic sink bowl; and fold-down pipe-cots took the place of comfortable seating around a table.

Rigs, too, became ever lighter but without the engineering to keep them standing. It didn't matter that they broke. The owner was there to buy a replacement. Rig failures became a common occurrence and my record in Sydney–Hobart and Fastnet races was not a good one as a result, with 50 per cent ending in retirements mainly through rig failure of one sort or another. I got to dread being wakened in my bunk by the sudden lurch upright, the loss of motion and nasty slamming, followed by the call 'All hands on deck'. We would rush up with bolt croppers and hacksaws in hand to cut away the broken spars before jagged edges had the chance to punch a hole through the hull.

Running dead downwind became a dangerous occupation in a big seaway, but we did it because that meant gybing less often than our rivals and a shorter course. With the introduction of fractional rigs, gybing too became an occupational hazard, particularly in strong winds. A regular cause of lost rigs would be when the mainsheet trimmer failed to get the mainsail pulled in amidships in time for the leeward runners to be wound in hard before the gybe, and another cause was those accidental Chinese gybes when the mainsail whipped across uncontrolled to become pinned hard against what had previously been the windward runner.

Boats became increasingly lighter thanks to the introduction of composite materials such as Kevlar and carbon that added exponentially to building costs. Keels became thinner, and in the quest to keep the ends of the boat as light as possible, the construction of rudders became just as suspect as that of the rigs. All this was experimented with on an expediential basis with too little thought given to the applied sciences required in metrology or composite engineering. Builders, designers and mast manufacturers relied totally on what had worked before and lightening it ... until something broke!

The yachts grew more and more ugly. Once-graceful cabin tops were replaced with square boxes slapped on the deck almost as an afterthought simply to meet the minimum headroom height set within the rating rules. As the boats became increasingly complex and the roles on board more specialist, including the job of steering them, owners invariably became less relevant other than to write the cheques and place their bulk on the weather rail. Better governance by the Offshore Racing Council and stricter control over the rules might have encouraged more sensible boats and led to better investment for their owners. Instead, they had to virtually give their boats away at the end of a very expensive season.

Failings and foul weather

I was one of the victims of these inherent structural failings during the infamous 1979 Fastnet Race when an Atlantic storm swept through the Western Approaches to sink five yachts and cause the loss of 18 lives. I was racing aboard the Ron Holland–designed

Irish Admiral's Cup yacht *Golden Apple of the Sun* owned by Hugh Coveney – the colourful Irish businessman and politician who became involved in the Good Friday Agreement that led to peace in Northern Ireland and who died in mysterious circumstances. He was a great supporter of Irish ocean racing and one of many owners to eventually walk away from the sport he loved. Much to his excitement, we had just led the fleet around the Fastnet Rock when the rudderstock on *Golden Apple* snapped – a fate suffered by four other yachts that year. Our race ended with us abandoning ship and being lifted off by helicopter.

These were horrendous conditions, but I have endured worse during past Sydney–Hobart races when the southerly 'buster' combines with a strong southerly tidal set to produce horrific 'wind against tide' conditions. Because there were no strict scantling rules to control construction methods, the yachts designed to the old International Offshore Rule (IOR) were simply not strong enough. I experienced this during the 1985 Sydney–Hobart Race on board Peter Whipp's Philippe Briand–designed *Panda*, which had won that year's Fastnet Race. We were full of hope and doing well in this second classic until the hi-tech core in the hull laminate sheered in the bow area and forced our retirement before we had even crossed the Tasman Sea. The prognosis was pretty clear-cut: there were not enough ring frames within the hull to withstand the pounding in those heavy, steep seas.

It was not the first time that I had experienced this. I competed in several ¼ Ton Cup championships with my German Flying Dutchman rival Ulli Libor, the first in Breskens in the Netherlands aboard the steel-constructed prototype of the *Listang* production cruiser/racer. The hull was probably no more than 3mm sheet, and the ring frames inside were spot welded to the hull sides. We blitzed the fleet in the short races and led the standings going into the final long offshore race, which counted for treble points. All we had to do was finish, but a 30-mile (48km) beat in fierce wind-against-tide conditions very nearly became our undoing. The pounding was simply too much for the boat: the spot welds on the frames began to fail, and the bottom plating started to 'pant' with every wave. How long could this go on for before the hull plating failed?

We tried shoring up the hull, cutting down a spare spinnaker pole and wedging it between the hull and deck head, with little effect. We slowed the boat right down and just hung in there, allowing the tide to push us to the lightship we had to round. *Listang* made it, just, and with the rest of the race downwind in relatively smooth conditions, we went on to win the trophy. Looking back, this was the scariest race I have ever done, for had the steel plating fractured, the boat would have sunk like a stone, with us in it. Sure, we had a life raft to hand, but would we have had time to launch it in the darkness with such a big sea running?

This, my first world offshore championship, was quite a baptism, and on reflection we should have retired, as Paul Elvstrøm did some years later when the mast threatened to push through the bottom of his ½ Ton-design *Bes* while he was leading the fleet standings by a considerable margin during the final long offshore race of the ½ Ton Cup off Hundested, Denmark.

Ulli Libor on Rodney

'Our first offshore race together was the 1968 Quarter Ton Cup in Breskens when Rodney really impressed me. We did very well in the shorter races, and had only to finish the final long offshore race to secure the trophy. Going out to the start it was blowing a full gale and our problems began with the backstay breaking as we came out of the river. Rodney managed to fix it, but soon after the start I began to hear odd noises from below. No one else did, so we got on with pushing the boat hard upwind. But then the noises became more distinct and I went down below to find that the welds holding the 3mm hull plating to the ring frames had broken on the port side and the shell was flexing. This was a bad situation, and for the first time in my life, I felt the need to wear a lifejacket. I went back on deck and we discussed what to do if the boat sank.

I went back down below and ripped out the wooden interior and used this to shore up the port side supported by a spare spinnaker pole jammed between the deck head and the temporary boarding. But soon after we had to tack for the mark and within half an hour the problem had repeated itself on the starboard side too, and I had to move all the supporting woodwork across. We had to slow the boat right down, lost a lot of time on the fleet and we all got very tired. Suddenly, Rodney announces that he is going below to sleep. I thought: "Hell, how can he go below to sleep in this situation?"

Two hours later, Rodney came back up and said, "OK, I've had a good rest. Shall I take over the helm again?" I asked him, "How could you sleep down below in this situation? If the plating had opened up, we would have sunk in minutes and you would have been trapped below?"

"Oh, no," he answered, "I was sleeping on the life raft, and if the worst happened, you would have woken me up trying to grab it!"

We managed to get to the windward mark, and set off downwind without the spinnaker set, still surfing along at 14 knots-plus. Remarkably, we pulled through to finish third and win the Quarter Ton Cup, but when we inspected the boat later, I found that the bows had buckled so badly that the plating looked more like crumpled newspaper!

I saw another side to Rodney when we raced a production version of the same Quarter Ton *Listang* hull after it had been made to rate as a Half Tonner. The boat now had a huge rig, bowsprit and bumpkin, and was very fast in lighter conditions. We were competing in the 1970 Half Ton Cup staged off Sandhamn, and going into the last long offshore race, which counted treble points, we had a good chance of winning this World Championship too.

During the first long beat, we pulled out a huge lead on the fleet ... so much so that we arrived at where the weather mark should have been long before the mark boat arrived. We continued going to windward thinking that the mark boat must be ahead of us until one of the crew spotted a light 1½ miles (2.4km) astern and we realised that the mark had been dropped after we had passed by.

On our return to port, Rodney lodged a protest about the race committee. The jury dismissed his criticisms and with them our chance of winning the Half Ton Cup. It was a travesty and Rodney was furious at the amateur way in which the sport was being run at that time.'

The Half Ton Cup at Sandhamn in 1981 was not well organised, but at least the race officer was prepared to reconsider decisions. Many are not, believing that righting a wrong is somehow losing face. One of the inshore races was started in a very weak land breeze, but the race officer was so sure that the sea breeze would eventually overcome it that he set course in anticipation of this predicted wind change. The Swedish boats got going to take advantage of this local knowledge, something we were not privy to, and found themselves at the back of the fleet because the change happened far too late to affect the results. The race officer duly shortened course and we finished with a good result. However, when we viewed the results the following morning, it came as a shock to learn that the race had been thrown out overnight and would be resailed. The jury did, though, agree to reopen the hearing if there was enough support, and on appeal the race was reinstated, showing that one should always stand up for one's rights.

Then there are the failings within a crew. I've faced rivalry many times when people join a boat with quite separate agendas to the rest of the crew and spend their time undermining the teamwork within. I've also witnessed shouting matches, but outright mutiny? Only once. Afterwards, I came to understand why mutineers were often hung from the yardarm in Nelson's day. I could easily have done the same to Danish sailmaker Ib Anderson when he decided to jump ship during the 1978 Half Ton Cup at Poole.

We were racing the Ron Holland–designed Spanish-owned half-tonner *Iberian Shamrock* with Lord Ambrose Greenway, who was a very talented navigator, and two Spanish lads. It was a very competitive fleet, with Tony Bouzaid's Davidson-designed *Waverider* (the eventual winner) carrying New Zealand's hopes, and a couple of Stephen Jones–designed Hustler 32s, *Smokey Bear*, skippered by 505 World Champion Larry Marks, and Graham Walker's *Indulgence*. It soon became clear that while *Iberian Shamrock* could hold her own in light airs, we quickly lost out whenever the breeze filled in.

At the start of the short offshore race, Ambrose noted that while the tide was ebbing out of the Solent, the tidal chart showed that the main Channel ebb near the Fairway buoy, our weather mark, was flowing in a north-westerly direction, ie inshore. The rest of the fleet cracked sheets, expecting to be pushed southwards by the stream flowing out of the Solent, but Ambrose wanted to continue to hold up on the wind. The gap between us and the fleet continued to widen, and by the time we rounded the buoy the rest of the fleet was far to leeward. It took half an hour for the next boat to get round the mark, but early euphoria turned to dismay as the breeze freshened and we were gradually overhauled on the leg to the Shambles lightship off Portland.

Ib Anderson began to lose confidence in *Iberian Shamrock*'s ability to win the Cup. When we turned up to prepare for the final long offshore race the next morning and found her half submerged at her berth, he became convinced that our chances had sunk along with the boat. I was having none of it, and after rallying the crew and marina staff to lend a hand, we got her pumped out. I also managed to find some fresh cushions and provisions, and we crossed the start line just three minutes before the cut-off time.

The light weather now played into our hands and we soon began to reel in the tail-enders. By the time we rounded the first mark off Cherbourg we were back in the pack, and at the next mark off Brighton we were challenging for third place. This was a race we could win … until Ib Anderson suddenly insisted that he be dropped off in Brighton Marina. He knew that with his departure we would have to retire from the race, but he saw no point in continuing. He had bigger fish to fry back home in

Denmark, making sails for yachts competing in the Two Ton Cup a few weeks later.

Ib is a brilliant sailor. A prodigy of fellow Dane Paul Elvstrøm, he won the 1973 Soling World Championship but relinquished his chance of winning an Olympic medal by choosing to become a professional coach to the Spanish Olympic team. He ended up as chairman of North Sails Europe. His departure from *Iberian Shamrock* made me so angry I have never sailed with him again, but in mitigation, Ib, unlike myself, was a family man with small children and a sail loft to run, and both clearly took precedence over our ambitions to win this World Championship.

Navigator Lord Ambrose Greenway on Rodney

'The winning streak within Rodney's make-up came to the fore during the 1978 Half Ton Cup in Poole. We were racing with Danish sailmaker Ib Anderson on the Spanish-owned *Iberian Shamrock*, a boat that was supreme in light airs but something of a dog once the breeze filled in.

We had a mixed series, leading whenever the winds were light, then falling back in stronger conditions. Going into the final long offshore race we had to win to stand any chance of a podium place. So imagine our dismay when we arrived at the dock for that last start to find *Iberian Shamrock* had sunk at her berth. Ib Anderson and I were all for calling it a day but Rodney was made of sterner stuff. Somehow, he managed to get the boat raised and pumped out, and found dry bedding and provisions in time to reach the start line within minutes of the one-hour time limit after the gun had fired. Luckily, there was very little wind and the fleet was still just visible in the distance.

Rodney concentrated like a man possessed, and by the time we rounded the first buoy off Cherbourg he had us up with the tail-enders. By the second mark off Brighton we were back in contention with the leaders and now had everything to

---

play for with a good chance of taking the lead on the final leg back to Poole. Rodney was delighted, but the mood quickly turned sour when Ib Anderson suddenly announced that he wanted to be put ashore in Brighton Marina. Clearly, he didn't share our optimism and decided that it would be more profitable to get back to Denmark to make sails for another boat competing in the Two Ton Cup a week or so later. Rodney was furious. The two had a right ding-dong on the foredeck and almost came to blows, but Ib remained determined and we put him ashore, and so having "lost" a crew member, we were forced to retire. Rodney's mood remained black all the way back to Poole.'

My first Fastnet Race in 1973 was aboard Paul Elvstrøm's *Bes*, after teaming up with Eric Duchemin, who manufactured Elvstrøm Masts in France. I remember being woken up by a sudden thump and rushing up on deck to find that we had hit a rock while becalmed off Start Point. We had drifted inside the Mew Stone and had the lighthouse right above our heads, and Eric was muttering, 'Not my fault, I was only following another yacht!' There was very little wind that year and it took a whole week to complete the 603-mile (970km) course. We missed the Fastnet Rock completely, our first sight of land being the Irish coast. The only good breeze came when sailing back past the Fastnet on the return leg to Plymouth. Reefing the mainsail for the first time, we discovered that the wire halyard had developed a riding turn around the winch. The wire was jammed hard around the drum, and was a serious problem until one of us realised that we could unbolt the winch from under the deck. That solved the problem and we were able to clear the halyard before it broke.

Another offshore sailor whom I enjoyed competing with was the Irishman Butch Dalrymple-Smith, who spent many years as Ron Holland's right-hand man before becoming a designer in his own right. We sailed together in the One Ton Cup in Newport and the Quarter Ton Cup in Helsinki and shared the experience of the 1979 Fastnet Race. We have remained best friends ever since.

Butch Dalrymple-Smith on Rodney

'Rodney was always an interesting guy to sail with. Building up to a regatta he would be fairly normal, but on the final day before the first race he would go into an enormous twitch about something totally trivial. During the One Ton Cup in Newport, Rhode Island, I remember he wanted to have a dimmer on the stern light so that at night we could make it appear to the boats behind us that we were slowly pulling away. The theory according to Rodney was that the pursuing pack would try everything to hang on to our taillight and they would upset their own trim, lose concentration, go frantic and slow down. It became a matter of life or death that we HAD to have this dimmer put into the circuit.

In Helsinki, I remember telling the Spanish crew beforehand about the "Pattisson Twitch" and we became a bit worried that he seemed relatively Zen (by Rodney's standards). Was he, we asked ourselves, taking this regatta seriously? We were very relieved when he suddenly went nuts just before the first race over whether the folding propeller, which anyway would be kept shut with an elastic band during the races, was aligned vertically or horizontally. We hadn't put any mark on the propeller shaft inside the boat. Rodney became almost hysterical about how important it is to get it fixed in a certain way or else we would have absolutely no chance.

Rodney took his racing EXTREMELY seriously, and of course would not have any alcohol on board. Well, this was anathema to the two Spanish kids on board and for the long race they smuggled a magnum of red wine on board. On the final leg of the long race Rodney was absolutely at his best, we were leading anyway but he somehow managed to herd the other boats into a string astern, which was much more reassuring than having them spread out and able to potentially gain an advantage from a wind shift. He was on the helm for about six hours, intensely concentrating, while the rest of us took turns going below since there was not enough wind to need everyone on the rail. Needless to say, every trip below was an opportunity to take a sip of wine. Just before the finish one of the guys handed up the near-empty bottle and offered Rodney a swig. He damn near exploded and it was all I could do to calm him down and try to explain that we had just won the regatta so what was there to get upset about?

Much of his success was down not so much to sailing talent, which he had in spades, as to his intense concentration and the way he always looked for every tiny thing that might make the minutest difference to winning. Once he found whatever it was, it became a matter of absolute urgency. It HAD to be fixed. Somehow he never seemed so concerned over more extravagant problems like having to replace the mast just before a regatta.

After every race, Rodney could remember every single tack, gybe and wind shift. He has amazing recall. We'd be in a bar somewhere and he'd suddenly ask me, "You remember halfway up the second beat when *Fortune Hunter* was behind us and *America Jane* to starboard, why did we tack?" We'd have to sit down and rearrange all the empty glasses on the bar to represent the tactical situation, remember how the breeze had been fluctuating and conduct a complete post-mortem on a single decision (generally when subsequent events proved that it was not a smart call). He could do that for every single moment of the race.

When all I wanted to do was to have another beer ... but then I wasn't a champion, was I?'

Sitting on the weather rail drenched to the skin in bitter cold weather, and being fed the occasional snack bar and sandwiches is not my idea of fun. Fortunately, I was often steering, and the intense concentration this requires helped blank out the boredom of racing monohulls.

The power of food

Good food is an important ingredient for success, and one that is often overlooked during the constant search to reduce weight within the boat. Sailing on *Jade* in the 1985 One Ton Cup at Poole we carried the extra weight of a combined oven and stove aboard, but it was worth its weight in gold. While other yachts carried only a gimballed single-burner gas stove to heat up hot drinks and some of their crews had to contend with chemically heated food cans, washed down with salt water, *Jade*'s oven allowed us to prepare hot airline-type food. This gave us a huge morale boost that was a definite advantage over our main rival *Panda,* and others who had to be content with eating stale sandwiches while sitting on the weather rail. Oh, how they must have envied us during their second night at sea!

Shifting from monohulls to multihulls

The Admiral's Cup was at one time a very popular event. With three boats per team – large, medium and small – in 1989 it attracted 22 teams. It had an interesting combination of races, starting with the Channel Race, then a series of inshore races, before culminating with the Fastnet Race. The latter is always a fascinating event. Starting off the Royal Yacht Squadron Line at Cowes, the course takes the fleet out through the western Solent and down the Channel. This poses a series of challenges for the navigator to beat the tidal gates at Portland, Start Point, the Manacles and Lizard Point. The Fastnet Rock is always a wonderful sight, but on occasion quite a frightening one, especially in darkness and in the storm force winds we faced in 1979. Pantaenius, an extra turning mark introduced in more recent times, makes the rounding of the Rock that much safer, especially at night, cutting out the risk of hitting the rocks on the western side and colliding with other yachts approaching from the south.

Sadly, though, interest in the Admiral's Cup has died, the last one in 2003 when won by the Australian team. I was privileged to sail aboard Bob Oakley's 63ft Australian entry *Wild Oats* that year, my first experience of sailing a boat with a performance-enhancing swing keel. We enjoyed a really good series, especially winning the Wolf Rock long offshore race, the final event in that year's Admiral's Cup. Our rock-hopping and lobster-pot-dodging antics alongside Portland Bill and the Purbeck cliffs against a full spring ebb tide proved to be the tactical move that won us that race and lifted us to top boat in the regatta. It also led to the team pipping the Spanish for the Cup – the first time the Australians had won the Cup for 24 years.

These two Australian crews had been representing the Royal Prince Alfred Yacht Club in Sydney, and on their return the boys from *Wild Oats* and *Aftershock* were invited to a celebration dinner at the club. Since I was in the UK, the organisers invited me to pen a few words. By then I was truly converted to the excitement of racing multihulls and wrote: 'I greatly enjoyed racing with Bob and his crew aboard *Wild Oats* … but if you really want to get a fast boat, then get rid of that swing keel and add floats!'

It was Peter Whipp's brother Mike who first introduced me to the joy and sheer exhilaration of racing multihulls. I had gone down to Exeter to see Larry Woodall's yacht *Jade* taking shape in a shed and was rather taken by the 60ft trimaran alongside her that Adrian Thomson had designed for Mike. *Paragon*'s hull had a foam core sandwiched between two layers of Kevlar/carbon hybrid cloth, and turned out to be one of the lightest, strongest multihulls of her era.

This led to an invitation to race on her against the top French boats in the Trophée des Multicoques regatta at La Trinité-sur-Mer in Brittany. She was fast straight out of the box, not only beating all her 60ft-Class rivals but also running rings round the 80ft multihulls, too. Her performance was so dominant that one French newspaper headlined our victory as 'Trafalgar at La Trinité'. I was hooked. My first opportunity to race her again came during the 1986 Round-the-Island Race. It was the 50th edition and *Paragon* marked the occasion by flying round its 60-mile (96km) distance in 3 hours 55 minutes 28 seconds – a record that remained unbeaten for the next 15 years!

The boat proved almost unbeatable until catastrophe struck while racing for an E-type Jaguar, the coveted prize for the first to finish in the 1986 Silk Cut Multihull Race between Brighton and St Katherine's Dock, London. The course took us north of the Dover Separation Zones and the dangerous Goodwin Sands, and around Galloper lightship, before entering the Thames Estuary.

As we closed on the Dover Straits with the wind right on the nose, I was steering *Paragon*. There was a strong force 5 easterly blowing, and with wind against tide, she was pitching horribly. The trimaran had been designed to carry a light carbon wing mast, but after running out of building time, an aluminium spar weighing almost 3 tons had been substituted for it – nearly twice the weight of carbon. It was this additional weight that was causing this terrible motion now, bringing us almost to a standstill at times. Nevertheless, we were vying for the lead with the French 75ft trimaran *Fleury Michon VIII* skippered by Philippe Poupon, which would go on to break the transatlantic record the following year.

Suddenly, a shackle securing *Paragon*'s mainsheet, the block-and-tackle device that controls the boom and maintains headstay tension, exploded with a bang. The shackle was rated to cope with a safe working load of 6 tons but had sheared through metal fatigue. Miraculously, none of the parts hit anyone as they flew out of the cockpit. We were off Dungeness and our trimaran was hobby horsing horribly in the pitch darkness, so it took a while to fix. By the time we were ready to set off again, we were well back in the fleet, in the presence of the smaller and slower Formula 40 catamarans, a new class that was proving all the rage at the time.

There was another problem, too. The drive belt controlling the rotation of the wing mast was now slipping badly, and because the wind vane was set on the masthead, our instruments were now wildly inaccurate. This didn't matter so much while we were beating upwind because we had a floodlight aimed at the wind telltales on the jib to steer by, but it would when we turned the corner and were running downwind into the Thames Estuary. Then, we would need to know the exact bearing of the true wind in order to decide the best route through the numerous banks, and whether or not to set the asymmetric spinnaker.

As we approached Galloper lightship, the turning mark into the Thames, I suggested that the best way to resolve the problem would be to steer dead downwind immediately after rounding the lightship to get an accurate reading from our main steering compass on wind direction and allow Mike, our navigator, to make the best tactical call. All went to plan, and we gybed the boat on to what was a fast reach.

A few minutes later, I became aware of another boat to weather and astern, going considerably faster than us, and converging on our course with her asymmetrical kite set. We found out later that this was the American Formula 40 catamaran *Team Smythe*, skippered by Tornado gold medallist Randy Smythe, which had cut the corner while we had been steering downwind. I had noticed back in Brighton Marina before the start how ridiculously small her bow lights were. Recessed into the front of her floats just a few feet above the water, these lights were now almost totally obscured by the fine spray and spume flying off her bows as she raced towards us at speed. Visibility was 8 miles (13km) or more that night, and the fact that we had spotted her only at the last minute emphasised the problem. Little did I realise the high price we would have to pay very shortly after for their lack of visibility.

I bore off a fraction, and without the kite we slowed right down, allowing *Team Smythe* to pass to weather of us, before resuming our course once more. Seeing her flash past was both exciting and alarming, but nothing compared with what was to follow!

A little later, while still sailing without our spinnaker set, I sighted a merchant ship some distance away on our port bow, approaching rapidly. She was moving left to right, showing two forward steaming lights (more than 150ft (46m) in length) and a green navigation light. Our speed was varying between 12 and 18 knots in the gusts, but her bearing was always moving right, so I was confident she would pass across our bows, probably quite close. I lost sight of the ship almost immediately after our paths had crossed and said to one of my crewmen, 'Take a look at the ship, she is close.' Judging the range of any ship at night with the naked eye is never easy, especially in the conditions we were facing, but I had spotted the reflection of her stern light on her wake and was confident that we would pass safe astern.

Water was flying everywhere in *Paragon*'s cockpit, with the worst coming from the leeward side, not that different from a power shower. Suddenly the crewman cried out, 'My God, she's coming straight at us!'

In that split second, I saw the bows of this ship looming out of the dark high above us just yards away and instinctively swung the wheel to port. It was too late to avoid the collision of course, but that change of course probably saved us from being cut in half. The ship's bows ploughed straight into the front of our starboard float. There was a huge jerk and then, just as suddenly, we were free again, rattling down her starboard side. Reflecting afterwards, I concluded that our leeward cap shroud must have hung up on the ship's starboard anchor, before then breaking free.

Down below, the impact catapulted Mike from the chart table into a bulkhead. Oblivious to all that had been going on, he now rushed on deck clearly in a state of shock. Fortunately, the rig was still standing but lunging around in a drunken manner, and we leapt to get the sails down. The two front beams had sheered on impact, but moulded with Kevlar cloth – a wonder fibre used for body armour – they were semi-connected, hanging like hinges. This undoubtedly saved the rig from falling down. Both cap shrouds were still intact, but attached to the floats. If the rear beams failed, then the floats would break too and bring the rig down around our ears. We struggled to lash ropes around them as fast as we could, bracing the lines tight with the winches, and eventually stabilised the damage.

Meanwhile, Mike got a distress call out on Channel 16 and told us that the Ramsgate lifeboat was on its way. Also standing by was the car carrier *Autobahn*, but there was no sign of the ship that had hit us. She had fled into the night.

Several hours went by before the lifeboat came alongside, and the coxswain with his mate jumped on board shouting (probably a well-rehearsed spiel), 'I'm the skipper … I'm in charge … Just give me the wheel,' before floundering comically on *Paragon*'s trampoline netting that filled the gap between the main hull, the beams and what remained of our floats. I almost added, 'And that's an order!' but then thought better of it. Moving around these nets with any confidence is an art at the best of times, and especially so in total darkness. I've often wondered since what our new 'skipper' must have thought at the time. I'm almost certain he had never commanded anything like *Paragon* before. We were lucky survivors for sure, and fortunately uninjured, but actually we were only requesting a tow!

Eventually we did arrive in Ramsgate harbour and, utterly exhausted, fell asleep on sail bags below. Next morning we examined the damage. The starboard float had peeled back like a banana as far as the front beam. Fortunately, the point of impact had occurred just ahead of a solid watertight bulkhead, which had kept *Paragon* afloat.

Interest now centred on the numerous dark green chippings found all over the deck. This was not matt anti-fouling, but glossy topside paint, which would provide a great clue as to what had hit us. There were other clues, too. Seconds before impact with the ship we had glimpsed, albeit briefly, a yellow derrick, lit up by the forward steaming light as the vessel swept past, and had also noted her superstructure right aft and a square transom. As to size, we reckoned on 2,000 tons, compared with our 8. As we built up a picture of what had happened, the full realisation dawned on us of how lucky we were not to have been impaled on her bows – with their watch keepers blissfully unaware of hitting anything!

In those days, insuring multihulls, especially for racing, was very difficult, and *Paragon* was no exception. The only way owner Mike Whipp could possibly recover anything was to find the ship that had hit us. The International Regulations for Preventing Collisions at Sea (COLREGs) are clear: on the open sea, power gives way to sail. However, without modern aids such as the now-compulsory automatic identification system (AIS), finding our rogue ship and proving she had hit us was going to be very difficult indeed.

Our first visit was to Dover Coastguard, which monitors the Dover Straits 24 hours a day and keeps a trace of all shipping movements. They calculated that the vessel was most likely to have come from Ushant and that her course close to Galloper lightship indicated an East Coast destination and not the Baltic. This gave us a glimmer of hope.

Merchant ships are required by law to file their movements with Lloyd's Register, but it often takes them several days, so we simply had to sit and wait. Eventually we had the printout we needed, and up-to-date times of sailings and departures of all shipping around the UK coast. Searching all ports along the East Coast by car would take too long; the only possible solution was to charter an aircraft if we were to have any chance of catching our ship before it sailed again.

By chance, John McWilliam, a respected sailmaker and keen sailor, came to our aid. He had served in the armed forces and graduated as a Red Arrows pilot in the RAF aerobatics team. I had sailed with him several times and knew he still had his own plane. Learning of our plight, he was eager to help. We rendezvoused at an Essex airfield and took off to start our search. It was going to be rather like looking for a needle in a haystack, but at least we had those clues. Having called up local harbourmasters and shipping agents, we already had a few green suspects to check. I was surprised by just how cagey they were when asked for a hull colour, as well as by how many merchant ships turned out to be green.

Viewing all the quays in a port and even an entire estuary took only minutes from the air as we worked our way up the East Coast, but it was only when we were over Middlesbrough that we found our first suspect. Size, shape and colour matched perfectly. As we circled round two huge cooling towers I was glad we had John as our pilot. Clearly, he didn't seem to be aware of low-flying restrictions, or simply didn't care! He took us low enough to read the ship's name – *Pyrgos*. The printout informed us she was carrying a cargo of potash loaded in the Canaries.

But there were many more quays to check first, and we continued flying north. Another similar ship was at anchor off Blythe: right colour, right size, obviously waiting for a berth, but no, she had come from the Baltic, so we could safely rule her out. We flew right up to the Scottish border, but with no more sightings we became more and more convinced that we had found our culprit, and returned to land at Middlesbrough Airport at dusk. Calling a taxi, we drove to the wharf we had circled hours earlier. It turned out to be the ICI wharf, right at the top of the river, and the vessel was still there, berthed portside-to. We needed to view her other side. We asked a few questions and learned that she would not be sailing that night, so early next morning we were on the other side of the narrow river looking straight across through our binoculars. It was no good, we needed to be nearer, but as luck would have it, we then stumbled on the harbourmaster's private dock. After he'd heard our story he agreed reluctantly to help us. His harbour launch, fitted with smoked-glass windows all round the cabin house, was perfect for the job and we headed upstream to take a closer look, The crew were offloading cargo, but the first officer spotted us, and did what every first officer would do – leaned over the side to check the ship's Plimsoll line. He needn't have worried on that count; after all, they had been unloading for many hours.

We turned round upstream and returned to pass by once again, this time almost at touching distance. To our huge relief we found the evidence we were looking for. There, as plain as daylight under her starboard anchor, inches above her waterline, was *Paragon*'s very distinctive yellow paint. One call to Mike's lawyer and the ship was arrested.

The collision had occurred during the middle watch, traditionally manned by the third mate. He knew it had been very close, but was sure, or certainly hoped, that he had missed us. As for our emergency call, maybe Channel 16 on the bridge had been turned right down, or even off. Fortunately for us, he never got to tell his captain about the incident. Had he done so, an unscrupulous skipper could so easily have had the telltale yellow markings painted over while anchored offshore waiting for her berth,

It turned out that the ship was German owned with a Maltese crew. The owner having denied all liability, the court case would have taken two years to hear, but fortunately another case was cancelled and our hearing was brought forward. Knowing that the game was up, the German owner agreed to settle out of court.

From the statements we read it appeared that very soon after crossing our bows the *Pyrgos* crew had spotted something straight ahead of them. It was of course *Team Smythe*, barely visible with her poor lights. In order to avoid that collision the helmsman swung the wheel hard to starboard, only to come straight into *Paragon*. Had there been a court case the outcome might have been very different, with the blame falling on *Team Smythe*, which was unlikely to have had insurance cover. Fortunately for Mike, insurance was compulsory for *Pyrgos* and they finally paid up.

This wasn't the end of *Paragon*'s career by any means. We formed a syndicate to purchase the wreck and had her repaired. Sadly, none of us was able to secure the sponsorship needed to campaign her and eventually she had to be sold, but not before gaining a successful charter: French yachtswoman Florence Arthaud sailed her in the Single-Handed Trans-Atlantic Race, sporting a new lightweight carbon mast. Sponsored by Groupe Pierre Premier, she finished a credible fifth despite suffering a broken boom. This was a heavy aluminium spar, which she managed to throw overboard – quite a feat single-handed; it always took five of us to lift it!

We finally sold the trimaran to French yachtsman Francis Joyon, who renamed her *Banque Populaire*. Now, three decades on, this remarkable trimaran is still racing. She has ten transatlantic crossings under her belt and has won line honours in the Heineken St Maarten Around-the-Island, Marion–Bermuda, Marblehead–Halifax Ocean, and Around Long Island races without ever inverting.

Record setting

I came back in contact with Francis Joyon in 2001, joining him and Philippe Colville aboard their 60ft trimaran *Eure et Loir* to attack my own Round-the-Island Race record set on *Paragon* in 1986. Conditions were perfect, and we skated round in 3 hours 8 minutes 29 seconds – an average of 19.1 knots, and a record that stood unbeaten until 2013.

In August the same year we set our sights on the Fastnet Race record. My success rate in this race is really very poor – worse than 50 per cent. Having started in seven of these 608-mile (1,126km) classics from Cowes out to the Fastnet Rock and back to Plymouth, I've only finished in three of them, the first in 1973 aboard Paul Elvstrøm's ½ Tonner *Bes*, when we were beset by light winds and the race took well over a week to complete. I was sailing aboard Hugh Coveney's *Golden Apple of the Sun* during that fateful race in 1979 when the rudder stock broke and we were forced to abandon ship; and the other three races all ended with dismastings. Yet the invitation to do the race aboard the 60ft trimaran *Eure et Loire* was not one I could refuse. The aim was to beat the previous best race record set in 1999 by Loïck Peyron in another French trimaran, *Fujicolor II*, which had set a time of 1 day 16 hours and 27 minutes – an average of 15.08 knots.

This was my first experience of offshore multihull racing and it opened a new chapter in my sailing career. We started in a full gale and poor visibility as we tacked down the Solent battling for the lead with the only other large trimaran in the race – Emma Richard's *Pindar*. Giovanni Agnelli's 90ft monohull *Stealth*, along with Ludde Ingvall's 86ft maxi *Nicorette* and various Volvo 60s were soon left in our wake and from then on posed little threat to our line-honour ambitions – provided we finished. Innovations such as water ballast and swing keels had improved the performance of monohulls significantly but multihull design had made similar strides, too. Wider, stronger carbon beams, lighter and taller carbon masts, some with hydraulic rams to pivot the spar, together with hydrofoil boards in floats were advances that made more powerful multihull platforms with the ability to carry increased sail area. Designs like *Eure et Loire* were still the fastest sailing craft around, and also the most exciting.

Starting with a storm jib set and two reefs in the main, we soon overtook a badly balanced *Pindar*, which was suffering from having too big a headsail and a smaller three-reefed main. She was carrying a crew of seven, and I felt quite sorry for them; after all, where would they sleep with only two berths below? We had similar accommodation on *Eure et Loire* but only numbered four: Francis Joyon, skipper and owner; Thomas Coville of Vendée Globe fame; myself as navigator; and a friend who had come along for the ride!

Once we had passed Poole Bay we held on out to sea to avoid the overfalls close to Anvil Point and St Albans Head before tacking for Portland Bill. The tide was still with us and when we were almost within touching distance of the Bill itself the water was amazingly calm. Some 100 yards (91m) further out it was a different matter, with really wicked overfalls running that would most likely have left us with broken gear at the speeds we were doing.

Dusk fell as we headed into the shelter of Lyme Bay, and with visibility improving we picked up the shore lights of Lyme Regis and Beer. The wind had begun to ease so we decided to shake out a reef in the mainsail and change to the bigger, more powerful No 2 jib. As I was about to learn, the speed of the sail change is critical. Watching Joyon and Coville do this on their own was a revelation. They dragged the new headsail on deck and, leaping about the nets, made the change in no time. Their trick was to have us luff the trimaran head-to-wind, which set *Eure et Loire* on a backward track of 5 knots. Without green water flowing over the deck and with much less motion, the task took half the time it would have done had we still been tracking to windward, even slowly. On a multihull it is far more important to complete the sail change quickly and get the boat back to full speed than to try to hold your position.

I'm not the best navigator in the world, so having one of the first Garmin handheld GPS sets, with its hinged aerial pointing skywards, was a constant asset. But these were still pre-chart plotter days and without a detailed chart showing the Skerries Bank off Dartmouth we resisted the temptation of seeking the lee of Berry Head and instead headed out into the Channel, since the tide was with us and the sea was now relatively flat. We finally tacked on to port well clear of Start Point and laid a course to pass just north of the Eddystone Rocks. An hour or so later we were closing on St George's Island off Looe in Cornwall and it was time to tack once more. We had been going for 12 hours now, and though we had been tacking all the way, I was surprised that we had already covered 160 miles (257km). But with another 450 miles (725km) to go and only 28½ hours left to beat the record, I was beginning to think this was a lost cause.

The wind was still from west-south-west and we eventually arrived off Land's End at midday on the Monday. Visibility had worsened and there was plenty of shipping around. We could hear their engines and fog signals but seldom saw anything, so kept a very good lookout with one of us stationed on the bow at all times. As we entered the Irish Sea there was a change in the weather that allowed us to ease the sheets for the first time and blast our way across to that famous rock.

The leeward float foil was lowered for the first time, and *Eure et Loire* began to fly, clocking speeds close to 30 knots. Water began to spray and my oilskins proved totally unfit for the task. Fortunately, someone had loaned me a wetsuit top, which I was wearing underneath, so at least my top half was dry if nothing else. It is no coincidence that fishermen tend to wear the old-fashioned PVC oilskins because seawater is unable to penetrate through these, and even if they get ripped, repairing them, although the result is often unsightly, is easy enough to do. At least any dampness within was only body sweat, and the colder it got, the more I could wear underneath.

Eating hot food was proving impossible. The gimballed single-burner stove could cope with coffee, tea and soup, but little else. I was left looking forward to a smoother ride back from the Rock and perhaps a proper meal at some time or another!

Visibility improved temporarily, and we spotted the Rock from 4 miles (6.4km) out. At these speeds of course, 1 mile (1.6km) takes about three minutes, so from seeing the Rock to rounding it all happened within ten minutes. Thank goodness, I thought, for a simple handheld GPS set that made finding marks in these conditions relatively easy. When doing this race in the ½ Tonner *Bes* we missed the Rock completely, then, finally sighting mainland Ireland, had to look for it again.

We rounded the lighthouse at 19.30. There were no committee or spectator boats to observe us, but the keeper gave us a wave and told us over the radio that we were first to round. We hadn't seen *Pindar* since leaving the Solent, but learned later that halyard failure had caused her crew to retire shortly after the Bridge buoy.

As we altered course to close-hauled, visibility closed in again and we began the 7-mile (11.25km) beat to the Pantaenius turning mark, laid specifically to keep arriving and returning yachts clear of each other. The problem was trying to find this small yellow buoy in the conditions. We headed away on starboard tack knowing that we weren't quite laying the mark, and watched the GPS display of our track and the bearing of the buoy as it slowly moved right. The nearer we got to the mark, the faster it moved right, until suddenly it was on our beam, and we tacked. There was a frantic cry from Thomas Coville, steering high up on the port beam, saying he could see the buoy and was trying frantically to bear way, and not hit it! We dumped the mainsheet traveller to relieve pressure on the helm and, with visibility now less than 50 yards (46m) or 7½ seconds at 12 knots, thought how lucky we were to have found it at all.

The ride back to Bishop Rock was anything but comfortable. The south-easterly course and freezing breeze barely made any change to the motion of the boat and our speeds were even faster than on the way out. Never mind: if we kept these speeds up, the record would be ours, and a hot meal and sleep suddenly became unimportant.

Sadly it was not to be. Two hours before rounding Bishop Rock the wind began to ease, and despite shaking out the reefs and setting the bigger Solent jib, we began to slow. As we approached the Lizard and then Plymouth, we passed many of the smaller yachts, their race having barely started, and perhaps they envied us, knowing we were just an hour or so from the finish, a shower and a decent meal!

All hopes of breaking the record were now over, but we still moved relatively fast with the masthead gennaker pulling us forward. Tacking downwind towards the Plymouth breakwater was so smooth and glorious compared with the pitching and slamming on the outward leg and back towards Bishop Rock. The wind came and went in bursts and it amazed me to see how *Eure et Loir* could generate its own breeze. Gybing through 90 degrees, the track was not dissimilar to going upwind, but in the opposite direction. Sailing too low an angle slows the boat quite dramatically, and the only way to rebuild it is with a hard luff. Sailing to the best VMG is absolutely vital. As we crossed the line at about 10.30 on Tuesday morning, a gun marked our time for line honours – a little under two hours behind the record.

Before this experience, I had never accepted the famous Olympic words of Baron Pierre de Coubertin: 'The important thing in life is not victory, but the contest. The essential thing is not to have won but to have fought well', but on this occasion they suddenly made sense. Standing under a cold power shower, and robbed of sleep and proper food, we had battled away for some 21 hours. For me, it was an experience of a lifetime, well worth every minute, and one I would never forget.

If the strong winds had freed earlier the record would have been ours, but that's ocean racing. There was no time to wait for the prize-giving that Friday. Both Francis and Thomas had to return to their home port of La Trinité-sur-Mer. Just as well, really, because out of the 40 or more trophies presented, there was none for Francis to collect. No cup for first round the Fastnet Rock, no cup for taking line honours, no cup for first multihull to finish, despite an £800 entry fee for the Race. Rolex, the main sponsor, could hardly have been proud of this, but it still took a decade or more for the Royal Ocean Racing Club (RORC) to recognise multihulls in any meaningful way. Their world revolved around monohulls, and multihulls were treated as interlopers. The silverware for line honours that year went instead to the first maxi yacht, which finished more than 24 hours behind us, and we had to make do with a consolation bottle of the sponsor's champagne!

It is all very different now. Rolex has undoubtedly had an influence on the race organisers, who now recognise the commercial and media benefits of giving multihulls an equal platform with monohulls. The result was shown in the 2015 race when 12 multihulls took part, led home by Dona Bertarelli and Jann Guichard's spectacular 131ft (40m) tri *Spindrift* which, under the previous name of *Banque Populaire V* skippered by Loïc Peyron, set the fastest time to date of 32 hours 58 minutes – an average of 18.5 knots – 12 hours better than the fastest monohull!

Though *Eure et Loir*'s Fastnet win went unrewarded, our performances encouraged the IDEC Group to sponsor Francis to go for the solo non-stop circumnavigation record two years later. He chartered the 89ft (27m) trimaran *Sport Elec,* which had previously taken 71 days to win the Jules Verne Trophy for the fastest outright time with a full crew. Remarkably, Philippe took just one day longer to complete the same distance alone with sails that were ten years old and without a weather router ashore providing advice. This was a truly remarkable performance, since Joyon cut 20 days off the previous solo circumnavigation record, and I was in such awe that I rushed down to Brest to welcome him back and present him with my first Olympic gold medal.

Joyon went on to break the New York to Lizard west/east transatlantic record, and in doing so also set a solo 24-hour speed record of 543 miles (874km). Unfortunately, he then chose to continue on back across the English Channel to his home port in Brittany, rather than stop and rest overnight at Falmouth. Exhausted, he fell asleep at a critical moment and his trimaran ran up on the rocks at Pointe de Penmarc'h, France and was wrecked. Joyon lived to fight another day, and the publicity he received prompted IDEC to fund another trimaran – this time purpose-built for single-handed sailing.

On 27 November 2007, he and *IDEC 2* – designed jointly by Nigel Irens and Bernard Cabaret – set out to recover his solo circumnavigation record taken by Britain's Ellen MacArthur two years before, and returned on 20 January 2008 with a new time of 57 days, 13 hours, 34 minutes. This cut almost two weeks off MacArthur's time and is still regarded as one of the most impressive feats in modern sailing history – so impressive that I felt duty-bound to ask Dame Ellen MacArthur to present him with my second gold medal as soon as he stepped back on dry land!

I had another memorable experience with Francis racing *IDEC 2* in the 2008 Round-the-Island Race. Bringing his multihull to Cowes, he had a double mission: first, to defend the Round-the-Island Race record we had set in 2001 with his 60ft (18m) trimaran *Dexia Eure et Loire*; and second, to return my Olympic gold medal.

I sailed my own small and comparatively humble F-27 trimaran single-handed up from Poole on the Friday afternoon and was pleased to see that *IDEC 2* had arrived overnight and was now on a mooring outside Cowes harbour, too large to lie alongside a marina berth with so much traffic, and with an early start the next day.

We woke early on Saturday morning to find just a light north-west wind, which was forecast to freshen during the day and shift to a south-westerly sea breeze later, when we would be on the south side of the island. We opted for a reduced crew of six and offloaded our small screacher and some surplus gear into the rubber dinghy. Even on a giant multihull like *IDEC 2*, every pound saved counts.

I felt quite privileged to be invited to be navigator and tactician for the day. I remember in 2001 asking Francis to enter all five turning points in the GPS. He wasn't very technically minded in those days and said *'Peut-être j'aurai la difficulté'* – 'I might have some difficulty with that.' I was amazed and asked, 'So how do you navigate across the Atlantic?' *'Beaucoup plus facile, il y a seulement deux points d'entrer, le départ et le finis'* – 'That's much easier. There are only two points to enter – the start and the finish.' I think he was joking!

This time I was somewhat relieved to see a chart plotter on board. I didn't want to be responsible for piling *IDEC 2* on to the rocky ledges south of the island. Of course, her 15ft (4.6m)-long carbon daggerboard would be the first to suffer, followed by her very slim rudders (taken off *Dexia Eure et Loire*). Fortunately, the rudder on the main hull had a sacrificial fuse to save the foil in the event of hitting a floating object.

Climbing aboard at 05.30, I enquired casually how everyone had slept. *IDEC 2* is very basic down below, with just one fixed berth and a jump seat, a gimballed single-burner stove and of course a traditional bucket acting as a toilet.

'Very well,' replied Francis. 'No problem. We pitched a tent on the trampolines, which made the perfect bed!'

Six years previously, on *Dexia Eure et Loire*, we had started this race with some 200 or so other boats of various classes in a really strong south-east breeze. Trying to hit the start line on time, blast reaching at 25 knots, had been far too dangerous and we had elected to start about a minute late, hoping to find some gaps in which to weave through the fleet. I remember a 24ft (7m) traditional Cornish shrimper right ahead of us, their crew shouting at us in desperation, and it was only through good fortune that we missed them. Afterwards, I campaigned for multihulls to start first, which the Island Sailing Club reluctantly agreed to. But now, just six years later, this had been conveniently forgotten. We were back to starting behind a large fleet of monohulls again.

Fortunately, with only a light north-wester and a close-hauled course for Hurst Narrows, starting speeds were much slower, although *IDEC 2* could quickly get up to 15 knots upwind whenever a sudden gust of wind hit us. Everyone, it seemed, had gathered at the far end by the Outer Spit buoy, no doubt seeking the favourable bias on the line, the probable benefit of more wind on the mainland shore and the first of the ebb tide. Francis managed to make a brilliantly judged start and steered round the other boats, though generally the fleet seemed to part ahead of us, in an act of either respect, terror or bewilderment at the thought of being trawled up in *IDEC*'s trampoline nets?

As we headed down the Solent, *Leopard* – the leading 100ft (30.5m) monohull, which had been little more than a speck on the horizon when we started – was closing fast. Soon we were on our own, save for Extreme 40s around us. These open-deck dinghy-type cats are a world apart from *IDEC 2*. Given strong winds and rough seas, they head for home or risk the inevitable breakage or, worse, a capsize. Rounding the Needles well clear of that renowned wreck, the *Varvassi*, we hoisted the huge screacher and moved into top gear. As we tacked downwind, through angles of about 110 degrees, the wind began to freshen. Gybing in these conditions with relatively smooth water was easy. Care had to be taken handling and controlling the mainsheet traveller as it tried to fly across the huge aft beam, and the old sheet on the screacher had to be frantically overhauled by two of us as we turned. At least there was a vast area of netting to run across. I was surprised by just how much boat speed we lost during the turns, and we had to head about 30 degrees above course to rebuild the apparent wind, but as it rose, the wind angle shot ahead and the telltales on the screacher stalled, with us bearing off accordingly. Speeding along at 25 knots in these conditions, the ride was utterly smooth and dry, and you needed to look at the instruments to actually realise the pace we were setting. We soon overhauled *Leopard*, which was flying an enormous asymmetrical kite but having to gybe through bigger angles than us. She was going slower partly because of having to drag a heavy keel, albeit a swinging one, together with the weight of what looked to us to be a crew that numbered three football teams!

The Extreme 40s, on the other hand, were a different story. They had much the same VMG as us, but were tacking through higher angles with more speed and making gains by quicker gybing on every little wind shift, as they slowly pulled away from us.

> **VMG**, or **Velocity Made Good**, is the computed speed of a sailboat into the wind or directly downwind. A yacht cannot sail directly into wind and has to zig-zag or tack upwind, and similarly, though to a lesser degree, downwind.

West of St Catherine's Point we gybed almost too close to the cliffs while riding the strong eddy that is always there on full ebb. Fortunately, this wasn't a spring tide, so dodging the stream by sailing in close to the rocks was less essential. Passing the lighthouse, we ran along the south-east shore past Ventnor to Dunnose Point. This is the highest point on the island and, anticipating a giant lee, we gybed out to sea to avoid the calms. The Extreme 40s were all gambling on staying close inshore, under the cliffs, playing the calms, and in doing so, shortening their distance to the Bembridge Ledge buoy.

Then the wind began to back as the south-east sea breeze began to fill in. Behind us was an incredible wall of spinnakers across the horizon and fast approaching as they rode the new breeze. Ahead of us lay Bembridge Ledge buoy, but in an area of no wind. Training the binoculars on the eastern Solent, I could see a fresh north-easter blowing there, so the calm ahead of us was caused by the convergence of these two opposing winds. Gybing or tacking *IDEC 2* when becalmed is not easy. The full-length battens within her huge mainsail need quite a bit of pressure in order to reverse the curvature in the top half of the sail. When curved the wrong way this becomes a very effective airbrake! We found the only way to solve the problem was for four of us to run along the beam, pushing the boom against a stop to send a shock load up the sail.

We eventually broke through the calm, but not before a fair number of monohulls, including *Leopard*, had overtaken us. Her much heavier displacement and more manageable sails gave her greater momentum to shoot the calms. However, once *IDEC 2* had also picked up a fresh north-wester we soon overtook her again and went on to finish first among the large multihulls home. Had it not been for the Extreme 40s we might have gained line honours, too, but were these day racers really fair opposition? How long would they last sailing round the world?

It had been a great day's sail; frustrating at times, yes, but we were happy. The race record we had set on *Dexia Eure et Loire* remained unbroken, so still ours, and Francis had very honourably returned my favourite Olympic gold medal won at the Mexico Games.

Cruising in a multihull

My own interest in owning a multihull had come from reading a report on the F-27 trimaran, the first to be designed with folding arms by New Zealander Ian Farrier. Ian had just won backing from American John Walton, a founder of the Walmart supermarket chain, who financed the development and moved production to a factory in San Diego. The first of these, named *Super Fox*, set a race record in her first outing, winning the 1984 two-man Around Catalina Race, a feat she repeated again the following year. I made a transatlantic call to enquire about buying one, and finished up as the UK agent!

I was very enthusiastic, but the concept then of cruising in a fast multihull was, in retrospect, ahead of its time, and the dramatic story of one of these boats capsizing in the Needles Channel drove away whatever enthusiasm there was for these boats; confidence did not build until Ellen MacArthur broke the solo circumnavigation record two decades later. I still have my cherished

F-27 and competed in several Round-the-Island races in her, as well as cruising around the Solent and the West Country.

One effort I made to promote the class was to zip *Times* writer Libby Purves and her photographer on a cross-Channel shopping trip to Cherbourg and back to show what the F-27 could do in a day. It didn't quite work out as planned, but made for entertaining reading!

I saw the event as a brilliant *Top Gear*–type challenge to sail as fast as possible across the 60-mile (97km) stretch of the Channel, have a good lunch, and be back in Poole harbour before sunset. What could go wrong? Libby, whose sailing is much more old school, saw it more as an opportunity to dissect the character traits of an Olympic medallist, purchase some French delicacies on expenses, and store up enough anecdotes to spin to her grandchildren.

The day began at short notice with a late-night call from my friendly weatherman to tell me that the forecast for the morning was perfect for the challenge. Libby arrived in the black hour before dawn with photographer Sarah in tow carrying a camera bag big enough to sink the dinghy. 'Did she really need so many lenses. Think of the weight!' She sensed my thoughts and I saw her mentally willing her cameras to shrink. Libby described me as 'a scraggy nervous hawk, sniffing the wind'.

Having driven through the night to get to our rendezvous, Libby was keen to catch up on her sleep. The first I knew of her intentions was seeing her sloping off down the companionway into the aft cabin while I was grappling to hoist the spinnaker. 'No,' I shouted. 'She can't lie there. It will cause transom-drag.' Evidently, that was a new sailing term not used on her family's traditional cruising yacht. Grudgingly, she moved herself off to the main cabin and lay down on the weather berth, browsing through the F-27 manual to get to sleep.

When she awoke, we were already crossing through the traffic separation zones at quite a lick. To her, the ships looked very menacing, and matters were not helped by me relaying the story of *Paragon* being hit by one in the middle of the night. I changed spinnaker and our speed climbed effortlessly from 8 to

14 knots to make this a glorious sail. Libby was less impressed, comparing the boat's movement to that of 'a trotting camel with 6 legs'!

She described our route to Cherbourg as 'a yachtsman's favourite rut worn in the sea' and recounted her first experience, no doubt at a much more leisurely pace, when the skipper's hat blew off halfway and was delivered next morning in Cherbourg – one of his friends following two hours behind had spotted it dead on his bow.

As the morning wore on and we were prancing towards France, Libby tried to doze on the trampoline netting, only to be woken with a start by a gallon of water rising up to soak her jumper. I don't think she was impressed.

By 13.00 we were off the outer breakwater and pondering the currency exchange rate. Libby suggested that we should have filled the boat with Cooper's Oxford Marmalade, tartan-tinned shortbread and Lancashire sausages, and set ourselves up in the marina as 'Le Marché Anglais' to raise money for crêpes et bolets (crêpes and mushrooms). It was Sarah, still brooding over my comments about the size of her camera bag, who reminded Libby that multihulls are speed machines, not cargo carriers.

Nor could she understand the rush around the supermarket and subsequent trolley charge back to the boat to catch the tide. We left late, and as a result lost the wind in the evening dusk. She, I guess, expected us to fall back on an iron topsail, but there are no such wind-cheating gizmos on this F-27 flyer, and we wallowed in the flat oily calm with Cherbourg's breakwater still very much in the picture. An ETA back at Studland of 21.00 soon became midnight, then 02.00, by which time the two *Times* women had fallen asleep, assisted by the stash of wine we had bought earlier in the day.

I woke Libby at 05.30 to glimpse the perfect dawn and marvel at the nifty performance of the F-27 even in these light airs. She was not impressed. We crept past Old Harry Rock at around 07.00 and I had them back on Studland Beach before 08.00, leaving them to wend their way home looking as if they were returning from an all-night bash.

Libby Purves' version of 'The Bet'!

'For a mildly timorous, middle-aged cautious cruising yachtie, there is a certain dash in being able to narrow one's eyes reminiscently, shake a grizzled head and say modestly, "Yep, I sailed with Rodney Pattisson!" Even better if I add, "It was one of his tightest challenges."

For indeed it was. Some years ago, with six world titles and three Olympic medals behind him, he challenged *The Times* newspaper with a bet in the tradition of Phileas Fogg: that, using a revolutionary small folding ultralight trimaran, the F-27, he could get under sail across the Channel (the wide 60-mile bit) to Cherbourg, shop, have lunch, and get back – all in a summer day, thanks to its 18-knot speed and his skilled determination.

Knowing my nautical predilections, *The Times* tasked me with witnessing this. I was on standby for about a week while Rodney conferred with his tame meteorologist, and at last the word came (I felt at the time it was rather like the moment in *Ben-Hur* when the bare-chested charioteer says, "This is the day, Judah!"). Unfortunately, I had people to supper and a play at the local theatre – in Suffolk – the night before, so opted to drive the six-hour journey to Studland beach overnight. I found Rodney pacing up and down by a vinyl dinghy, with his girlfriend Jane and Sarah the photographer. Bleary-eyed, I saw just offshore this extraordinary craft: a sort of arthropod (the folding idea was that the outriggers bent up like a grasshopper's elbows to save width when trailing). It was too late to quail at the thought of challenging the Channel in that. So at first light we glided out, hitting five, then seven knots without really noticing. I yawned, and Jane kindly said I should have a nap in the stern cabin.

"No!" cried Rodney, appalled. "She'll cause transom-drag. Windward bunk – main cabin. We load these boats like aircraft." I dozed off, careful not to move or turn over to upset the delicate trim; wedged against the centreboard case, I felt our speed rise, clattering as if on cobbles. The only similarly jerky experience I had ever had was on a trotting camel in the Sinai desert. We were doing eight knots, in eight knots of wind. Sleepily, as I woke I registered terrifying bygone reminiscences from the helmsman's chat: "... big green bastard, I said my God he's going to hit us, just a glancing blow, float peeled back like a banana..." As the wind rose, he abandoned the helm to anyone handy so he could skip around changing spinnakers at high speed (how many of the damn things were there in that float?). Occasionally as he tightened a sheet, he would bark an expression we have used in our sluggish old monohulls ever since, whenever we grind a winch – "Accelerating – now!"

So we were. We bounded onwards in a rising wind, and as I lay on the windward net, waves began to rear up and soak me. We skimmed, thrummed, leapt towards the Cherbourg peninsula, Rodney cursing any freighter which forced him to leave his track. We women lounged, admiring. Sunhats blew off.

By one o'clock we were there. Cherbourg! Jane began murmuring raptly about some special cheese called Epoisses de Burgogne she had her eye on. Sarah took more pictures. Cherbourg smelt, as it always does, wonderfully of *boulangeries*, Camembert, chips and dodgy drains. It was hard to believe we had done it so fast.

But it was not a time for leisure. There was a bet on. England again by sundown, with a full meal served! And when we reached the huge *supermarché*, Rodney accelerated again, taking charge of the trolley, jinking, barking "come on!" and cornering round mountains of dogfood tins like a kamikaze Go-Karter. Jane observed that he always moved that fast, and tends to eat his meals as though the 5-minute gun has just gone off and everything must be finished by the starting signal. Rodney barrelled across the cobbles back to the marina, and hurled the food aboard, to be laid out on deck for Sarah to photograph from the masthead as an elegant feast. Rodney thought the shopping was worryingly heavy, looking with particular suspicion at a vast can of *soupe aux poissons*.

Sixty miles home, and a fair reaching wind forecast. Easterly, force 4. But the Channel does not give up easily, and in moments we were in a flat, oily calm, looking at rather too good a view of the French coast over the gently bobbing stern. Our ETA was 9pm. Then 10. Then … well, there was wind at last. A light headwind. We girls finished off a bottle of cheap 70p wine along with plenty of baguettes and the remnants from the photographed feast and then slept as night fell. Rodney did not sleep. Working every zephyr, every puff, he steered through the darkness. At 0530 in the morning he woke me to admire the windward performance of the F-27 in light airs, and I went back to sleep, agreeing with him. One tends to. Just before seven we crept back to Studland past Old Harry himself (I could have sworn he laughed), and I braced myself for the six-hour drive home to deliver copy for *The Times*.

The great man lost his bet that night. But as I wallow gently in our cruising boat at 5 knots, or drift pointlessly round on a Topper on the River Alde, getting in the way of the Dragon fleet, I can still say the magic words: "Yep, I tried for a world record with Rodney Pattisson. And if it hadn't been for the weight of that damn soup, and I suppose me too…"'

FOUR

America's Cup

The America's Cup took over my life between 1982 and 1983. I was lucky because those two years were the most significant in the long history of the Cup, with Alan Bond's wing-keeled wonder *Australia 2* breaking 132 years of American dominance. The British challenge, led by the buccaneering Peter de Savary, turned out to be the most competitive in the entire history of UK forays for the 'Auld Mug', and had we not been faced against one of the most radical designs, our own *Victory '83* might well have been the boat to break what was the longest run in sporting history.

Peter de Savary, or PDS as he likes to be called, had provided some last-minute financial support for Tony Boyden's British challenge in 1980. *Lionheart*, Boyden's black-hulled Ian Howlett design, had shown some promise, especially when equipped with a radical bendy rig that added 100 sq ft (9.3 sq m) of 'free' mainsail area. My old rival John Oakeley had been her original skipper until replaced by a young Lancastrian dinghy champion, Lawrie Smith – the youngest person ever to skipper an America's Cup yacht. She lost out to Alan Bond's *Australia*, which in turn went down 4:1 to the Dennis Conner–skippered American defender *Freedom* in the Cup races.

De Savary's small investment in *Lionheart* gave him a front-row seat at Newport, and he liked what he saw. First, he knew that he could improve on the hapless management that had led to so many failings within the *Lionheart* campaign. But, more importantly, it gave him a golden opportunity to sit at the same table as some of America's most powerful entrepreneurs. And to this deal-hungry banker then living in the tax-free haven of Nassau in the Bahamas that was too good an opportunity to pass up.

Americans love showmen, and PDS certainly gave them the full Barnum & Bailey circus routine. The 38-year-old public school drop-out had what was described by one writer as 'a fondness for huge Havana cigars, headlines, fast cars, fast boats, his own opinions, and winning – not necessarily in that order. One syndicate had a faster boat, but no one left a larger wake.'

He arrived in Newport a full year before the Cup leading a major amphibious assault involving four 12 Metres, 100 personnel, a sea plane, a helicopter and a floating command centre in the form of the beautiful 140ft (43m) vintage motor yacht *Kalizma* that once belonged to Elizabeth Taylor, together with a veritable fleet of support craft. He couldn't have made a bigger splash and Rhode Island tradesmen rubbed their hands in expectation.

The campaign had begun two years before with a plan to build a core team around an Admiral's Cup offshore racing challenge. De Savary, who knew very little about top-level racing at this stage, became heavily influenced by the Lymington yachting set. Though challenging for the America's Cup through the Royal Burnham YC in Essex, he was persuaded by his good sailing friend Kit Hobday to commission Lymington-based designer Ed Dubois to produce the 40ft (12m) ocean racer *Victory of Burnham*, and for dinghy champion Phil Crebbin to pull in a top team around him to sail her.

She appeared to be a fast boat – very fast – and she played a major role in securing the 1981 Admiral's Cup Trophy for Britain. This also carried de Savary on a wave of euphoria to retain the same team to lead his *Victory* America's Cup challenge. At the time, Harold Cudmore and I were racing on a rival boat, *Marionette*, owned by Chris Dunning. We were dumbfounded by *Victory*'s performance and were left scratching our heads over how to try to beat her. Like most things that appear too good to be true, once the plaudits had been accepted and the boat put up for sale she was proved to be just that: *Victory of Burnham* had been racing a full 1ft (30.5cm) below her real handicap. Her measurement rating was incorrect and everyone, including designer Ed Dubois, swore they had no idea. The man who measured her was made the scapegoat.

De Savary, who was ignorant of these shenanigans, marched on undaunted by the scandal, commissioning Dubois to produce the lines for *Victory '82*, his flagship America's Cup challenger, despite the fact that Dubois had never designed a 12 Metre yacht before.

PDS also bought up the remnants of the *Lionheart* campaign, together with *Australia*, the Ben Lexcen design that had beaten *Lionheart* in the semi-finals of the Louis Vuitton Cup to determine the ultimate challenger for the 'Auld Mug' in 1980. Harold Cudmore and Crebbin were appointed to command afterguard and they took off in 1982 to establish a base in Newport and start training in earnest.

Thanks to Harold, I was invited out on two occasions that year as 'guest' helmsman to provide some competition on the trial boat. It was a steep learning curve. Racing a heavy 12 Metre yacht displacing 26 tons is a world away from Flying Dutchmen dinghies and even the offshore racing yachts at the time. A 12 Metre has to be coaxed up to speed and tacked with care to keep the momentum going. Throw them around like the J24 dayboats used in match racing championships at the time and they would simply stop in their tracks like stubborn mules.

Harold Cudmore on Rodney

'I've known Rodney since he was in his prime, though have to admit racing against him in the Flying Dutchman Class was a bruising experience. Focus and commitment are the two words that best describe him. Like Winston Churchill and General Montgomery, Rodney is a warrior and if I was running the UK and needed someone to fire a torpedo to save the nation, I would give the job to Rodney – but wouldn't necessarily invite him round for dinner afterwards!

I had the good fortune to meet his father, who had the same wiry stature and intense personality, and who of course did do just that: disabling the *Bismarck* with a torpedo fired from his Swordfish during World War II.

During an Olympic year we had very little interaction with Rodney. He became so focused on winning a medal that he went into a zone of his own. Precision is a major part of his personality and he could become impervious to any social interaction. There were those who didn't know him who were easily offended by his directness, when he would think he was doing the correct thing. I remember us sharing a car to drive to a party during a European regatta. We were all pretty broke in those days and agreed to share the petrol costs. No sooner had we arrived than Rodney calculated the exact amount and cost of petrol used down to the last penny and proffered his share!

Extreme success invariably leads to a war zone running somewhere in the background because his victories engendered equal jealousy and resentment in others. One example was when the Italian Federation invited Rodney to compete in a regatta and tried unsuccessfully to use the excuse of paying his travel expenses to get him excluded from the Olympic Games for being a professional. While the public respected his abilities and achievements, there were a lot of people out to get him, and as is the case for any successful politician, it became a quite a burden to carry, and Rodney always had to be on his guard.'

Midway through that year, Rank Xerox stepped in to sponsor a special 12 Metre race around Newport and de Savary decided to bring *Lionheart* out of mothballs to join *Victory '82* and *Australia*. He duly contacted her designer Ian Howlett and her former skipper Lawrie Smith, and I got a call from Harold Cudmore to see if I would join the fun.

Lionheart was a mess. Some of her deck gear, including winches, had been half cannibalised and her sails were out of date. Lawrie and Ian did a good job in getting her back together, and much to Harold's consternation, I chose to sail with them, even though they were rank outsiders.

Discouragingly, we were given *Victory '82*'s reject sails, but despite that, we came very close to beating her boat-for-boat. PDS was most impressed, and much to the chagrin of Crebbin and Cudmore, invited Lawrie and me to join his challenge.

We did not bring good news. Ian Howlett, a brilliant yacht designer who had lived and breathed 12 Metres since his student days at the University of Southampton, told de Savary that *Victory '82* was no more legal than *Victory of Burnham* had been. That came as quite a shock. To bring the boat back into measurement required major surgery, chopping off a large portion of her stern, which would have the effect of reducing her waterline length and performance.

Worse, we told de Savary that neither Lawrie nor I would join the team unless he ordered a new boat. He said there was simply no time to do this, but Ian, who already had a new design worked up, knew of a builder – Allday Marine in Southampton – who could construct the aluminium hull in record time; and on that basis, *Victory '83* was born.

Lawrie and I finally joined the campaign in time for winter training in Nassau with *Australia* and *Lionheart*, and quickly learned de Savary's modus operandi – rule and divide! We were pitched into a series of match races against Phil and Harold. Lawrie relished the competition and we worked well together, with Lawrie doing the starts and windward work, and me steering on the downwind legs. If nothing else, this gave Lawrie the chance to have a smoke! It became open warfare, with the other side taking control of the best sails and sailors. Swapping boats between rounds of match racing, we, the supposed underdogs, did really well and, afterguard apart, team spirit within the camp rose sky high.

Peter Bateman, who with Julian Brooke-Houghton had dominated the Fireball Class before graduating to the Flying Dutchman, was freshly appointed as team coach, and coped remarkably well with keeping the war contained, though there was one occasion when it was necessary to repel boarders. We were involved in 'dipping' practice, an exercise requiring particularly good communication between helm and bowman, when the give-way yacht has to dip the stern of the starboard-hand right-of-way boat. The latter used to tow an inflatable mark for the dipping yacht to round to avoid collisions, but Lawrie, determined to make the closest dip of the day, finished up T-boning *Australia* on the port quarter.

When two 26-ton 12 Metre yachts come together it is like two rhinos rutting: one is going to come off much the worse for wear. Luckily no one was hurt, but the damage was so extensive that it took a week to weld *Australia* back together again, and the impact 'sprung' her mast. PDS was furious and I learned a valuable lesson in understanding the huge kinetic energy involved with these heavyweight boats, as well as the importance of having clear communication from stem to stern.

The gruelling build-up

Our daily routine began at dawn, starting with a physical training programme. If we were not racing, the rest of the day would be spent two-boat tuning and testing new sails, just as I did during my Olympic campaigns. North Sails UK, managed then by Iain MacDonald-Smith, was sending sails to us as fast as we could test them and I shuddered at the thought of what they might be costing. Just humping them on and off the boats each day was enough, though being shorter than most of the crew lessened the pain because I was always taking less of the weight.

Given one day off each week, we amused ourselves as best we could. The palm-fringed sandy beaches around Nassau might seem like paradise for a week, but after a month, the scene pales considerably. For a while, the *Victory* boys became the most frequent customers at The Waterloo Club, the only nightclub on the island. With a bar at one end and a beautiful floodlit pool at the other, it didn't take long for guys to think up a challenge to link the two.

One evening, John Thompson, one of our grinders who could never resist a bet, stripped naked in the bushes and plunged into the pool. He then swam the length submerged and surfaced briefly at the far end to down a piña colada before swimming back and escaping the attention of the nightclub bouncers. He did it to great applause, but the next night a sign went up saying

'ABSOLUTELY NO SWIMMING' and soon we were all banned from going there.

The Club Med holiday resort on Paradise Island was another good venue with free entry, until one night a *Victory* crewman burst on to the stage riding a motorbike. That was followed by the sail truck incident when Russell Pickthall lost control, with the open back full to bursting with *Victory* crew members, and hit a tree, catapulting some over a fence into a compound guarded by vicious dogs. The police had to be called to their rescue, but of the driver, there was no sign. He had already been carted off to hospital!

When PDS questioned all this behaviour, Lawrie Smith answered characteristically: 'Well, what do you expect us to do in the evenings in such a shitty place?'

The only time this crew took anything seriously was whenever a stranger joined the team. So divisive was de Savary's 'rule and divide' management that new faces were always treated with great suspicion. Any new arrival invariably signalled that one of our number would be leaving shortly. Everyone had got used to my beard, which I had grown two years before to hide the facial scars sustained in a motorcycle accident during a regatta in Porto Cervo. It was far too hot for beards, so I quietly shaved it off. The next morning, I skipped the early PT session and arrived deliberately late for breakfast, sitting down at a distant table. The animosity was instant.

The ruse didn't last too long, for while most had never seen me without a beard, Iain MacDonald-Smith gave the game away. A few days later when PDS returned from a business trip, I caught him, too, asking who I was!

By April 1983 the weather was improving in Newport, and we decamped from Nassau. Lawrie and I had done well, beating Phil and Harold most of the time. Cudmore was worried that he might be out of a job and decided to hold de Savary to ransom. 'Either you name me as skipper or I leave,' he demanded. Much to Harold's surprise, he was thanked for his services and shown the door. Cudmore's sudden departure also left Phil Crebbin's position as a co-skipper in jeopardy because Lawrie and I had begun to work really well together and there was never going to be room for three skippers on the boat.

Lesson learned: don't challenge leadership unless the odds are overwhelmingly in your favour.

As *Lionheart* and *Australia* were being towed the 1,000 miles (1,600km) back to Newport, we returned to England for the launch of the new boat, *Victory '83*. As Princess Michael of Kent swung the champagne across her bows, she was launching our hopes that, finally, Britain had a competitive boat not only that could take on the six other challengers from Australia, Canada, France and Italy, but with which we could finally challenge the Americans.

De Savary led us back to Newport with the razzamatazz of a circus showman. The *Victory* syndicate was first of the challengers to set up camp and our numbers soon swelled to more than 100. He created something of a British oasis, to the extent of shipping over my Morgan and accepting a fleet of Aston Martin 'staff' cars to go with the British Bulldog motif embroidered on our crew clothing.

His attention soon focused not on our immediate rivals, but on the defenders. Tom Blackaller – who had the Hollywood good looks, charming smile and flowing silver locks that turned heads – was discounted as a 'good time' guy who would never get his act together sufficiently to get to a position of defending the Cup. It was Dennis Conner, a two-time winner with a first-class inferiority complex, who became the bogeyman. Conner covered his personality issues with hard work, long hours and meticulous preparation, and de Savary employed every method above and below the belt to unsettle him.

Every day when his *Freedom/Liberty* group went out to practise they found themselves shadowed by a small British rigid bottom inflatable (RIB) manned by a camera crew recording every minute. The buzz of the RIB's outboard got under Conner's skin and on one occasion he sailed 20 miles (32km) across rough open water to the other side of Block Island to shake off the boat. When that didn't work, Conner trailed monofilament fishing line from the back of his two 12 Metres in the hope of snagging the propeller. The support crew tried firing a warning shot across the bows, but not even deliberate rammings could knock de Savary's snoopers off their task.

The Americans complained that they had caught us Brits nosing around their workshop. We fed rumours that a series of outboard engine problems had been the result of sabotage, and that the Conner camp had alerted the FBI in the hope of getting our immigration cards suspended.

De Savary revelled in all the press attention that this phoney war was generating, knowing that he had found Conner's Achilles' heel – a chronic lack of self-assurance.

Robert McCullough, a former commodore of the New York YC, now head of its America's Cup Committee, tried to intervene, asking de Savary to stay away from Conner. PDS casually blew cigar smoke back in his face, saying that he intended to do anything and everything within the rules to win the Cup.

McCullough went away empty handed and the following day the *Victory* RIB went out as usual, armed this time with a handheld satellite dish to be used, Conner assumed, to eavesdrop on their private communications. When he returned to the dock, the American exploded when he spied another satellite dish sited within the British compound aimed directly at his polished aluminium caravan known as the 'Oval Office'. Barry Pickthall happened to be there to interview Conner for *The Times*, and bore the full brunt of Conner's scattergun angst aimed at all Brits in Newport. Interview over, Pickthall went to the *Victory* compound to get the other side of the story, where shore boss Andrew 'Spud' Spedding revealed these 'listening devices' to be nothing more than broom handles attached to silver-painted dustbin lids! De Savary was delighted.

Looking up skirts

Once the Louis Vuitton Challenger trials had got under way, Alan Bond's *Australia 2* scored ten wins from as many races. We knew she had a wing keel but, like everyone else, had no detail. Ian Howlett had been testing various winglet ideas conceived by the model boat designer David Hollom, and had gone to the lengths of getting a confidential ruling from Alan Watts, the chief measurer at the International Yacht Racing Union, that the concept was legal on a 12 Metre. The one proviso was that the winglets could not be adjusted while racing.

Derek Clark, *Victory*'s self-appointed design coordinator, wanted confirmation of what exactly was behind *Australia 2*'s modesty skirt, which had kept the keel hidden from prying eyes ever since she had been shipped from Perth. The Australians had tried to camouflage the appendage by painting it a two-tone blue, but the wings at least were quite visible to us whenever we were at close quarters to the yacht.

I had a friend who had left the Navy to set up his own commercial diving operation and de Savary agreed to invite him over to Newport. There were issues. If he brought over his own advanced apparatus which disguised the telltale trail of bubbles, he might have faced awkward questions at the airport. The same might happen if he tried to hire this equipment in the USA.

In the end, Derek took it into his own hands soon after the Australians had arrived in May, and secretly dived into their dock one night with Bill Bullard, leaving Graeme Winn to keep look-out from *Kalizma*'s support boat. De Savary, aware of the plot, threw in a word of caution. 'Please don't do it today because I'm having lunch with Alan Bond, but whatever you do after that is fine by me!'

Derek didn't take a camera in case the flash alerted armed guards pacing around the wooden dock above, and instead relied on finger touch to gauge its shape. What he felt must have been such a shock to his sharp scientific mind, I'm amazed he didn't expel a huge bubble of air in surprise. He found that the keel had been fitted upside down with a shorter cord length attached to the hull, a leading edge that sloped forwards, and with aerofoil-shaped wings protruding from the bottom aft end.

Derek and Bill resurfaced outside the dock to find no sight of their pick-up boat and quickly swam out of view of the Australian dock to surprise a Scandinavian crew eating dinner in the cockpit of their Ocean 60 cruising yacht by climbing up the stern ladder and peeling off their gear.

Crews from other syndicates began bragging around Newport that they too had spied on *Australia 2*'s keel, so 'Spud' Spedding and Russell Pickthall, *Victory*'s sailmaker, cooked up a 'chicken run' challenge to poke fun at all this over-hyped security.

There was only one rule: you simply had to return with a picture of the keel.

De Savary joined in the fun too. He decided to celebrate his 39th birthday on 11 July by squeezing one of *Victory*'s support boats into the dock next to where *Australia 2* hung in slings, then leaned on the boat's air horn and made a great show of peeping under the shroud. Shouting to the guards, he offered Mr Bond his best regards and suggested that he tighten up security, before roaring off in a cloud of cigar and diesel smoke.

Warren Jones, Alan Bond's strategist, failed to see the amusing side of this. 'They are driving us bananas. I can't believe it,' he proclaimed testily. 'Why don't they leave us alone to get on with our job?' Then he promised that anyone caught inside *Australia 2*'s modesty skirt would be prosecuted.

The *Victory* shore team had struck up a friendship with their opposite numbers in the Canadian camp, so it was not surprising when they too had a go at winning the 'chicken run' challenge. Unfortunately, one of their number got caught red-handed: at 5.30am on 22 July, the guards spotted two divers and managed to nab Canadian James Johnson, who was turned over to the police and had his camera confiscated. The incident caused a full-blown diplomatic row with the Canadian Ambassador in Canberra called into the Australian Foreign Office to explain. Warren Jones pressed trespass charges, and applied for a court order to prevent the film from being developed. That came to nought when Newport's city solicitor said he would have to develop the film and introduce the photos as evidence. Bond's strategist then dropped the charges in return for the undeveloped film and a formal apology from the Canadians.

Such was the fall-out that Spud Spedding and his opposite number in the Canadian camp put aside covert plans to swap boats round one night so that crews coming down the following morning would find *Canada 1* in *Victory*'s slings, and *Victory '83* in their dock.

The Canadians said it was all a joke – which it was – and we only learned later that their fulsome apology masked a much more professional attempt by Royal Canadian Navy divers to discover *Australia 2*'s secret. Bruce Kirby, *Canada 1*'s designer and 'Father of the Laser dinghy', wanted to know as much as us just what was under the Australian skirt. That was taken by others within the camp as a signal to organise a spy mission, and when a Royal Canadian Navy vessel made a courtesy visit to Newport, the team made contact. The ship's CO vetoed the idea, but a *Canada 1* crewman then approached the ship's frogmen privately and they agreed to swim in under the cover of darkness. By all accounts, they were better frogmen than photographers, and though they accomplished their mission unseen, the pictures taken on Bruce Kirby's camera proved useless.

Jostling for position

We know that the Italian team from *Azzura* did a spot of 'fishing' around *Victory '83*, but since our winglets could be unbolted, and were removed every night, it is unlikely that they saw much. Our winglets were beautifully cast in bronze and expertly aerofoiled. Small versions had been tested on models in the Wolfson tank at the University of Southampton and had shown marginal gains in performance, and, importantly, with minimal drag. Fitted to *Australia,* they showed a small improvement in performance to windward and helped tacking and manoeuvring considerably. Bearing in mind that a conventional 12 Metre tends to lose 3 knots of speed in a tack and takes 5 minutes to regain it, this was a very useful tool for match racing. So no wonder I was anxious to use them. Their angle of attack, however, proved critical. Just a few degrees out and they increased drag considerably. A lot more testing was required to fine-tune them, first on *Australia* and then on *Victory '83*, which had a different keel profile to our trial horse. Any chance to do this thoroughly was lost when PDS suddenly announced that he had sold *Australia* to Syd Fischer's rival Australian challenge, leaving us without a boat to trial against – not just these winglets, but also sails and changes in rig configurations. This undoubtedly harmed our programme, but the decision was taken in a drastic effort to save money by halving the burgeoning number of personnel within the *Victory* syndicate.

Development on the winglets was duly put to one side, but I felt Hollom's idea was worth pursuing and pressed for this research work to continue. If we could only get their angle of attack right, they might improve both *Victory '83*'s manoeuvrability and her upwind performance.

The only practical opportunity was in a race against the hapless Australian challenger *Advance,* dubbed the *'Down Underdog'.* She was so bad that one prankster arranged an appointment for her to visit the local vet. Her crew certainly had a sense of humour and, heartened by her first victory in 20 tries, undertook to paint the face of a dog on her bow, planning to add one feature at a time after each subsequent win. They never got further than the whiskers. We very nearly became this dog's first and only dinner.

The test was not a success. Phil Crebbin was at the wheel and became more and more depressed by his poor start and *Victory '83*'s sluggish performance. As his mood blackened it gradually spread to others on board. *Victory '83* had never performed so badly and during the final run Crebbin turned to me in frustration and shouted, 'You have a go!'

After settling the crew down again, we managed to take advantage of a couple of good wind shifts and got into a position to blanket *Advance*'s wind, and claim 'water' at the leeward mark prior to the final windward leg. It was then just a case of covering the Australians all the way to the finish to win by the closest of margins.

It was a lucky victory, and the forward crew vowed that they would never race with the winglets in again – not that this decision would ever be theirs. I said much the same about racing with Crebbin, telling de Savary and Lawrie that I would only sail with him again if Smith could produce a doctor's sick note.

Neither PDS nor Kit Hobday took me seriously. Kit, I learned later, told Peter that I would never leave the team because not only did I have my Morgan sports car in Newport, I had both my sister and a girlfriend living in Boston. That was a major miscalculation.

What I didn't know at the time was that Phil Crebbin's contract carried a clause stating that in the event of him losing his role as skipper, he would still have a place within the crew. Lawrie and

I discussed his mood swings at length and resolved that because of the adverse effect they had on the crew we would not have him on board with us again.

A few weeks later, my partnership with Lawrie was again split and I was called to race with Phil. I told Lawrie, 'I won't do it. I won't be out there,' and to de Savary's surprise, I wasn't. He radioed back to base asking where I was. 'Rodney's left, and given me a letter to hand you when you get back,' replied Jane, our crew manager.

I took off to stay with my sister Susan in Boston. A few days later, de Savary called me late at night to say, 'Crebbin has gone,' and to invite me back to continue sailing with Lawrie. I had learned from Harold Cudmore's sudden departure that you need to be on strong ground to challenge PDS.

A short time later, we suddenly found Chris Law thrust into the mix. He had enjoyed some success on the professional match racing circuit and had joined the team ostensibly as mainsheet trimmer. However, it soon became clear that Law had a second agenda – to be the starting helmsman.

This became all too apparent when Law and I were invited to join de Savary on his Magnum 50 powerboat to watch the start of an informal starting sequence and first beat challenge between *Victory '83* and *Australia 2*, our first opportunity to sail against her. Law provided a running commentary on the start and criticised Lawrie's every move, making it crystal clear how he could improve the boat's competitiveness. I listened in horror. He had not been much good as mainsheet trimmer, over-sheeting the sail before the boat had built up speed, thinking a 12 Metre could be thrown around like a dayboat.

When I told Lawrie, we resolved to show up Law's inexperience by organising a series of match race starts between us. He lost all six so comprehensively that we thought this would be an end to the matter. But no, de Savary continued to insist on having Chris meddling on board. His presence was so divisive that this led to another confrontation with de Savary. Having succeeded once, I was deputised to speak up on behalf of the crew: 'Are you telling me that if Chris doesn't go, then you do?' asked de Savary. 'Well, if you put it that way, yes,' I had to answer.

It took a day for PDS to mull it over. Unbeknown to us, Law had done a deal with him back in London that should he be sacked from the boat, de Savary would employ him for a year in a senior role in one of his companies. The first we knew of this was when Law returned to England to become managing director of a tri-skate company based near Portland.

Secrets and subterfuge

These confrontations within the *Victory* campaign were small beer compared with the controversy now swirling around *Australia 2*'s wing keel. By late July, her scoreline read 25 wins: 3 defeats. She was clearly fast, and the Americans still didn't know why. They had missed a golden opportunity to see the boat naked when the official measurers were running their tape over her, having omitted to put the date in their diary and hence failing to show up for the one free peek allowed.

Australia 2 was not only the most manoeuvrable of all the challengers, she could gain half a boat length's advantage with every tack, was faster upwind and down in any wind strength, and could point higher, too. She had some very clever sails designed by Tom Schnackenberg, the team's New Zealand sailmaker, who was first to come up with radial-cut headsails and mainsail and, much later, the Code 0 gennaker. But it was the keel that made the biggest difference. When skipper John Bertrand first saw a model of it at the test tank facility in Holland where designer Ben Lexcen had been developing the concept, he said in his book *Born to Win*: 'Holy Shit. How many times have I told Benny "Give me a similar boat to the Americans and we'll go out there and sail it better", and he goes and puts a rocket under my cockpit!'

With the shroud around her keel, the armed guards and continued secrecy – even though it was too late to make a copy – they couldn't have done a better job of psyching out the opposition. What was even better as far as Bond's men were concerned was that they had the public on their side, especially when the New York YC decided to try to eliminate *Australia 2* any way they could. First, they attempted to surreptitiously purchase the keel design from the Netherlands Ship Model Basin, the tank testing facility where the keel design had been perfected. When they were caught doing that, the committee tried to rule *Australia 2*'s wing keel as a 'peculiarity' and as such illegal under the 12 Metre Rule.

Peter de Savary was called to a clandestine meeting shortly before the Louis Vuitton semi-finals at which the Italian and Canadian finalists were present, but not Alan Bond. They were advised that the New York YC would support any protest from the challengers to eliminate *Australia 2* from the remaining rounds of the challenge trials. It was a clear attempt to drive a wedge between the challengers, but however attractive that might have been, de Savary, who had the confidential ruling from the International Yacht Racing Union saying that a wing keel was legal, felt it would be hypocritical to pretend otherwise, and declined to agree.

The Australians might have come unstuck here, for they had not thought to clear the keel design prior to these races. Their radical 12 Metre had been measured and ruled to be in class, and they had simply left it at that, without gaining an official interpretation from the IYRU. In a magnanimous gesture, de Savary came to the Australians' rescue by making public our confidential ruling on the *Victory*'s winglets, and the New York YC was thwarted once more.

We beat the Italian yacht *Azzura* in the semi-finals without the winglets on *Victory '83* but, knowing that we had to raise our game considerably if we were to beat *Australia 2* in the finals of the Louis Vuitton Challenge trials, I still wanted to test them once more, this time set to what we believed might be the correct angle of attack.

The only other boat with a known performance was *Azzura*, and I was deputised to ask Mario Pelashier, a former Olympic sailor, if his crew might help us. The Italians happened to have their ball that night, and I had to gatecrash the party to get a chance to speak to him. Though we had knocked the Italians out of the series, Mario very sportingly agreed to help, and a two-boat test was set up shortly after.

We didn't dare tell the crew. After the *Advance* incident they had threatened to go on strike if anyone even whispered the word winglets! Lawrie and I therefore agreed to keep it from them. We got 'Spud' Spedding and his shore crew to secretly fit the winglets that night and have the boat in the water ready to go early the following morning. Pacing *Azzura* upwind, we appeared to be a little faster and also quicker in turning, but before we could prove anything conclusively, Pelashier called up on the radio to say that something had broken on *Azzura*, forcing them to cry off any further trialling.

We wanted an impartial opinion, so on our way back to harbour, Lawrie and I asked everyone for their observations. Without exception, all thought that *Victory '83* had shown a marginal improvement. It was only then that we announced that we had been sailing with the winglets fitted, which led to a near mutiny. Kelvin Rawlings, the strongest voice at the front end of the boat, who liked to think he was spokesman for the crew, made it quite clear that they would not race with them again.

In fairness, the results had been marginal and the trial too short to draw any sensible conclusions, so we decided to face *Australia 2* without the winglets. But as that opportunity closed, another development arose from an unexpected quarter.

It was in America's interests that *Australia 2* did not proceed beyond the Louis Vuitton Challenge finals. Dennis Conner would have much preferred to face a conventional 12 Metre like *Victory '83* rather than the unknown quantity that Ben Lexcen's wing-keeled wonder represented. Robert Hopkins, an American coach who had taken over from Peter Bateman within the *Victory* camp, got a call from John Marshall, president and CEO of North Sails, who, more importantly, was also a senior member of Dennis Conner's afterguard. He offered advice on how to reconfigure *Victory '83*'s rig to improve her manoeuvrability against the Australians. The offer had clearly come from Conner and involved increasing headsail size, moving the mast back in the boat and losing some mainsail area. Although there was now very little time, this was achieved and the improvements were carried out. The cost was considerable and all credit should go to PDS for agreeing to do it. This made the boat better balanced and certainly helped her to tack quicker.

Sadly, this was not enough to beat *Australia 2*. We won the first race by just ten seconds, but only because we abandoned match racing practice and sailed our own race without covering our rival. If we had covered them in an effort to protect our early lead then we would have lost the race because *Australia 2* was so much more manoeuvrable, gaining half a boat length with every tack. Thereafter, skipper John Bertrand paid greater attention to outmanoeuvring us at the starts and won the Louis Vuitton Challenger trials 4:1.

With just two weeks before the start of the Cup match, the New York Yacht Club then questioned the nationality of *Australia 2*'s design. The rule governing the America's Cup at the time insisted that the designer had to be a national of the challenging country. Lexcen was certainly Australian, but what part had the scientists at the Netherlands Ship Model Basin played in the design of the wing keel? The New York committee had secretly sent a lawyer to investigate in Holland, where he had learned that Dr Peter van Oossanen – the head of the tank testing facility – and, more pertinently, Joop Sloof – his opposite number from the Dutch Aerospace Laboratory who was working on winglets for Boeing aircraft at the time – had been the ones to perfect the wing keel concept. The problem for the Americans was that neither scientist was prepared to sign an affidavit to confirm this, and without that proof, Australia's right to challenge for the Cup in *Australia 2* was upheld.

After we had been knocked out, Peter de Savary magnanimously allowed us to stay on in Newport to watch *Australia 2* beat Dennis Conner's *Liberty* 4:3, and take the Cup Down Under. It was an extraordinary event and the result continues to have reverberations around the world.

It remains a credit to de Savary's entrepreneurial skills that his *Victory* challenge remains the closest Britain has ever got in modern times to winning the America's Cup. He marshalled not only the best skills and resources but also the funding to put up a high-profile campaign that won unbridled support, from royalty right down to the man in the street back home in the UK. His showmanship put even PT Barnum in the shade and he had the media eating out of his hand. Perhaps the sport could do with more larger-than-life characters like him.

Peter de Savary on Rodney

'We managed to pull together the cream of British sailing talent, Rodney included, to challenge for the America's Cup, and I watched to see how they performed both individually and within the team. It soon became very apparent that Lawrie Smith and Rodney worked very well together in the afterguard and their combined talents rose to the top.

It was probably Rodney's training in the Royal Navy that made him such a good team player, and his skilled analysis of both situations and technical issues, coupled with his concentration levels when steering or calling tactics, made him such a strong asset.

It was unfortunate that the *Victory* '83 campaign should have coincided with Alan Bond's undoubted super boat, *Australia* 2, because had we faced a "normal" 12 Metre in the Louis Vuitton Challenge finals, I believe we had the boat and the crew to become not only the challenger, but one that would have gone on and beaten the American defenders for the first time in 132 years.'

Politics in sport

Boycotting and its legacy

Do politically inspired sporting boycotts have any effect? Who remembers the stand taken by the Netherlands, Spain and Sweden in boycotting the 1952 Games in Melbourne in protest against the Soviet invasion of Hungary? Who recalls Egypt, Lebanon and Iraq's boycott at the same Olympics over the Suez crisis? Those protests were lost on everyone other than the national team members who were so badly affected by these bans that they devoted the rest of their lives to making sure that their countries never made the same mistake again.

I feel exactly the same about the Royal Yachting Association's ban on British sailors competing at the 1980 Olympic regatta in Tallinn in protest at Russia's invasion of Afghanistan. I didn't approve of this aggression, but have always believed it to be far more effective to attend an event than stay away, and make your feelings known during the competition.

At the 1936 Olympics in Berlin, black American athlete Jesse Owens' record four gold medals did more to crush Adolf Hitler's populist myth about Aryan supremacy than any political stand or newspaper headline.

In 1968, black American athlete Tommie Smith won the 200m race in record time at the Mexico Games ahead of white Australian Peter Norman and fellow black American John Carlos. The three used their positions on the podium to protest against black discrimination, with Smith and Carlos displaying Black Power salutes during the national anthem. The coverage they received worldwide did far more to promote their grievances than any boycott.

My own efforts to highlight the injustice of Russia's invasion of Afghanistan during the 1980 Cannes and Hyères pre-Olympic regattas also had an effect within the sailing world. My petition to draw to the attention of Russian crews the fact that the rest of the world did not condone such aggressive behaviour left them shocked because such was the censorship of Russian news at the time that none of them knew of the invasion or of the attitude of the western world towards it. Three decades on, I still believe that this small protest did more to educate Russian sailors than the entire American boycott of the 1980 Moscow Games and the stand taken by the Royal Yachting Association in pulling the plug on Britain's participation at the Olympic regatta.

This mixing of politics and sport didn't make a jot of difference to Russian foreign policy, but it had a huge effect on British Olympic yachting. A generation of sailors who had dedicated their lives to the dream of winning a medal and spent many thousands of pounds trying to turn dreams into reality suddenly found themselves sidelined without a voice. Many very talented sailors just walked away totally disillusioned, never to return to Five-Ring sailing again.

The Olympic Charter requires national federations to resist all pressures of any kind – be they political, religious or economic. Boycotts have never worked in the past and we need to guard against politicians using sport as a weapon at future Games.

A gold for Chris Davies

Politics mixed with sport makes a murky mess. Controversial decisions are often taken anonymously, facts become distorted, and the truth is frequently masked behind the belief that there is 'no smoke without fire'. My fight to get Chris Davies his MBE following our gold medal victory in the Flying Dutchman Class at the 1972 Olympics is a case in point. He was the only Olympic gold medallist that year not to have been rewarded in the Queen's Honours system. Why?

It took me 30 years to lift aside the cloak of secrecy that shrouded the issue to discover the reason and another three to have this slight redressed with the help and influence of many people inside both political and sporting arenas. No one within government circles or the Civil Service was prepared to answer any questions, and the Royal Yachting Association, which should have been pressing for answers, if not for an award for Chris, did nothing for fear of upsetting the secretive world of gongs and knighthoods and, perhaps more importantly for them, the faceless Whitehall mandarins who administered the system.

Robert Philip, a sports columnist with the *Daily Telegraph*, was one of the few to ask questions. He wrote:

'If Rodney Pattisson truly is the greatest sailor since Horatio Nelson, then Chris Davies, his crewman in Munich where they won the Olympic gold medal in the Flying Dutchman Class, was his Sir Thomas Hardy. But whereas Hardy was honoured with a barony after the Battle of Trafalgar, Davies has been blithely ignored by an ungrateful nation.

"Since Harold Wilson decided that every Olympic champion should receive an MBE following the Mexico Games in 1968," explains Pattisson with tangible bitterness, "26 British sportsmen and women have won gold medals in individual or paired events – Matthew Pinsent and Andy Holmes, who partnered Steve Redgrave, for example – and all without exception have been honoured in this way. Except poor Chris, that is."

Pattisson, who received his MBE in '68 in the company of his previous crewman, Iain MacDonald-Smith, has been battling Davies' cause with the same determination and enthusiasm with which he used to battle the wind and sea while amassing two Olympic gold medals, one silver, eight world championships and four European titles. "In spite of numerous requests to two Prime Ministers, two Sports Ministers, the British Olympic Association and Princess Anne as President of the Royal Yachting Association, someone somewhere within the nominations department of the Civil Service keeps blocking Chris's honour. It's a complete and utter mystery. I was delighted to hear of the five English soccer players who finally received their MBEs 34 years late, but I would very much like to know what Chris has done to deserve being treated in this fashion," says Pattisson.

Perhaps Davies has a skeleton in his closet? A dastardly criminal record, for instance. "I've been racking my brains," confesses our latter-day Hardy, now 53 and a senior lecturer in yacht manufacturing technology at the Southampton Institute. "The best – or worst – I can come up with is a speeding ticket I got a number of years ago. But I've examined my conscience," he adds with a gentle smile, "and I'm quite prepared to stand up and be counted. I don't know, perhaps there is something I've done in the past which I don't think is important and they do."

According to those who have sailed with him, Davies is one of the most modest, decent and honest men to stand atop an Olympic podium. He was also a damned fine crewman, winning four of the first six races with Pattisson at the helm at the '72 Olympics and finishing so far in front of the rest of the armada that they could afford to skip the seventh and final race to begin their celebrations a day early. "It was obviously a very sad occasion, too, because of the slaughter of the 11 Israeli athletes. Fortunately for us, the Olympic regatta was held in the Baltic Sea resort of Kiel, so we were some way removed from the full horror."

Just as the forgotten World Cup five – Alan Ball, Roger Hunt, George Cohen, Ray Wilson and Nobby Stiles – thoroughly enjoyed their recent day out at Buckingham Palace, Davies admits he would relish the belated recognition. "I've had a lot of time to reflect and, looking back, the MBE would probably have been quite a secondary thing to me back in 1972. It would mean a lot more to me now because it's a lifetime later, isn't it? That said, while it's an honour I'd obviously be very pleased to accept, as a sailing person to be respected by someone like Rodney probably means even more than the gong itself. I don't want to belittle it in any way, but I'd put Rodney on a higher pedestal than the MBE. I have to say, this campaign is all driven by him, so I have no way of knowing the full amount of effort he has put in on my behalf."

Like Nelson, Pattisson has been firing off broadsides in every direction; letters, faxes, phone calls, including a plea to Sports Minister Kate Hoey. Like so many before, he has not received an answer. Pattisson, ever the renegade, is not about to accept "no" for an answer. "It's an outright injustice and I hate injustice of any sort. I accept it may have been a simple oversight in the first place, but why not admit that and honour Chris the way they've done with the footballers? I first made the RYA aware of Chris's case in 1984 and, quite frankly, they haven't been trying. Reg White and John Osborn, who won the Tornado Class at the '76 Olympics in Montreal, received their MBEs, as did Mike McIntyre and Bryn Vaile in '88. Even Jim Saltonstall who was the coach in Atlanta four years ago was honoured, so what on earth has Chris done wrong?

"Interestingly, quite out of the blue I had a call from a bloke in the Sports Council a couple of years ago who sort of hinted that he somehow or other knew that there was one civil servant whose attitude was that these things aren't necessarily automatic at all. Good heavens, if 26 gold medallists out of 27 isn't automatic, what is? Then last year I received a call from Simon Clegg of the British Olympic Association who told me: 'I've got news for you. I think it's going to happen ... I can't say what it is but there's a window of opportunity coming up.' Basically, I think what he was telling me was that with the millennium looming, the Government was going to rectify a few wrongs by maybe handing out more MBEs than usual. I said to him: 'I've heard all this before and I'm getting fed up with it. Every year I have a go and nothing happens.' Needless to say the Millennium Honours' List was published and Chris's name was missing again, which led me to think: 'What have the RYA been doing, if anything?'"

If Davies is the saint everyone claims – "Well, I'm clean, but not that clean," he grins – could the RYA be getting back at Pattisson for his buccaneering spirit? "Chris is hardly Kim Philby. Now it could be a classic case for not being awarded the MBE because I've made quite a few enemies in my time, but not Chris. I can't think of a nicer man in any sport and I rather fear the RYA reckons it all happened such a long time ago they think it can be forgotten. And they're frightened if it's not forgotten, people are going to say: 'why didn't they do something about it sooner? Why has it taken so many years?'

"Why indeed?

"With each year that Chris Davies' name was not added to the Honours' List, what might once have been excused as an oversight or uninformed error simply became a greater disgrace to the whole honours system, and I was asking 'Whoever has been blocking Chris Davies's MBE these past 28 years please step forward and explain yourself.' But no one ever did.

"It was only in 2002 when secret Cabinet papers were made public under the 30 Year Rule that answers were finally found. The issue related to an unexpected visit to the Kiel Olympic regatta centre on the part of Prime Minister Edward Heath to congratulate us after our gold medal success at the 1972 Games. Unaware of the visit, I had left the Centre. Chris, who, like me, had not drunk alcohol for two years, was in the bar imbibing a few celebratory drinks with his wife and family when Heath and his entourage walked in. It appears that Chris was a little over familiar in addressing the Prime Minister as 'Ted', who turned his back and walked out. The Cabinet Papers show a hand-written note, probably written by one of Heath's staff, saying: 'This man is not to be honoured in any way.'

"Once this was known, I wrote a letter to the *Daily Telegraph* to highlight this injustice and called once more for Chris to be awarded an MBE. This drew a response from Edward Heath, then retired, who defended the decision by suggesting that not all gold medallists had been honoured this way since the Wilson Government set a precedent in 1968. Heath, however, had made the mistake of including gold medallists from the Commonwealth Games, and after my riposte stating that ever since the Mexico Games in 1968 every Olympic gold medallist bar one had indeed been honoured in the Queen's Awards, his corner went noticeably quiet on the matter."'

Chris finally got his MBE in June 2005, but only after a massive social media campaign supported by Olympic champions and sailors.

Barred from running with the Olympic torch

There is no doubt that my straight-talking approach and single-mindedness has got me into trouble over the years. It's led to spats with race officials, Olympic coaches and my own national authority, which have led to some mind-numbing pettiness with regard to their responses. The worst was being snubbed as a torchbearer prior to the 2012 London Olympics when the sailing regatta was held in my home county of Dorset.

I was nominated by Parkstone Yacht Club to be one of 1,350 people to run 300m in Dorset as part of an 8,000-mile (12,875km) course around the UK, the names being judged anonymously for their inspirational contributions to sport, art, culture or community. I was not disappointed when my name failed to make the cut, believing that there must be others who were far more deserving than I. Questions only arose when I found that the torchbearer chosen to run along the bottom of my road was an African athlete who had never competed for Britain. How did he qualify as being more inspirational than someone with three Olympic medals to their name – and a British passport?

No one had any answers. The only response the *Evening Echo*, my local newspaper, could gain from the London Organising Committee of the Olympic Games (LOCOG) was: 'The selection judges were looking for nomination stories that had the power to motivate and inspire the watching world.'

I appealed to Lord Coe, chairman of LOCOG:

'Dear Seb

I am rather surprised that 2 Gold Medals and a Silver has not been considered as a suitable qualification to carry the Olympic Torch in Dorset, my home county, where the Olympic yachting event is being held.

I trust your own Olympic medal qualifications won't qualify you either, but that remains to be seen.

RODNEY PATTISSON'

Lord Coe replied, saying that with numerous nominations for each place, the choice was a difficult one. It was clear not every nominee could be chosen to carry the torch. He then continued with a suggestion that I might like to become a 'Local Leader' – organising an event for friends, family or the local community.

Jane then spoke to Ben Ainslie, who now matched my Olympic medal haul and had already been honoured with carrying the torch on the first 300m of its journey around the country. He contacted Sir Keith Mills, deputy chairman of the London Games organisation, who replied directly to Jane. His response was no more helpful. After explaining that decisions taken by the panel were final, he added: 'All nominations were judged and scored and those that had the highest scores were selected as torchbearers, based on the strength of their nomination story alone.'

Undaunted, Jane picked up her pen again and this time wrote to the Princess Royal, in her capacity as President of the Royal Yachting Association, to highlight the apparent snub:

'Dear Princess Anne

I do hope you get the opportunity to actually see and read this letter, knowing time is of the essence to you, being so busy and fully occupied with the numerous public appearances you make, whether for all your various Charities or other public engagements. Your constant and continued hard work is something I admire enormously.

In view of your considerable involvement in bringing the Olympic Flame to the UK, and having explored all other avenues without any success, I am now appealing to you as my last resort!

I am married to the Olympian Rodney Pattisson, who I know has had the privilege of meeting you on quite a few occasions in the past.

Of course you do have a couple of things in common; you are both ex-Olympians and you both enjoy the pleasure of sailing.

My husband, incidentally, is quite good at fighting other people's battles and defending good causes. For example, he spent 30 years trying to secure an Honour for his crewman Chris Davies after their win in Kiel in 1972. However, when it actually involves himself, he goes and hides in a corner!

Rodney was nominated by his local Yacht Club, Parkstone, to carry the Torch in Dorset. He has lived here most of his life, learned to sail in Swanage, won 3 sets of Olympic Trials in Weymouth and Poole, and of course the sailing events themselves are at Portland. Despite all this, he was firmly turned down. Apparently, he failed to earn enough points in the so-called anonymous selection process, supposedly involving selection panels across the UK, and as LOCOG stated to the Bournemouth Echo, who queried it, those chosen needed to "inspire and motivate the World".

In just the first week now of running the Flame, no less than 8 UK Gold Medallists plus 1 foreign, 5 Silver Medallists and several ordinary Olympians have had the honour; so I hope you will agree with me, it does seem strange and indeed rather unfair!

Incidentally, the torch will run just 100yd from our house, carried by a Hungarian, of which 8 others are doing the same in the rest of the County; the reason apparently, because it is a prime global event.

Incidentally, Ben Ainslie, appalled about this, and who has always stated that Rodney was his inspiration, has tried himself to rectify the matter; but, like others, came up against very deaf ears.

Another LOCOG excuse is that the Torch Schedule is now set in stone and nothing can be changed, but this is simply untrue! How come within a few days of Chelsea winning in Europe, Didier Drogba, the footballer, was running. And so too, was the DJ, Chris Moyles, who admitted afterwards that he and his team only knew 4 days before?

I do really hope that, in spite of your very busy schedule, you can find a moment to try to rectify this totally unfair and unjustified situation.

JANE PATTISSON'

Remarkably, the block on my participation was lifted within 24 hours, and I was allocated the task of carrying the torch into the Weymouth Olympic venue.

Jane Pattisson on Rodney

'By most standards Rodney and I married late. We met just short of my 40th birthday and Rodney had turned 50 the previous year and we were inseparable from the start. For Rodney, boats had always taken precedence over girlfriends. Both of us had a fairly unconventional streak and the daft notion that marriage was for other people. It took Rodney eight years to get around to sort of proposing. The nudge came when he attended his niece's wedding in America, and returned to my flat in London clutching a bedraggled bridal bouquet to give to me.

As this was a first for both of us, we decided on an unusual venue, the millennium-old tiny chapel on St Alban's Head overlooking the sea on Dorset's Jurassic coastline. We also had the offer of a fabulous house looking out over Old Harry Rock in Studland Bay to celebrate at afterwards.

Madly, I decided to do all the catering! Years of experience within the fashion and film world in London had given me sufficient experience to work hard the week before, then delegate the final tasks to a group of fabulous friends to allow me to relax and enjoy the weekend.

Not to be outdone, Rodney announced that he would be sailing to his wedding. Never mind the horrible legend of St Alban's Head in which a couple sailed away from their nuptials only to drown in the dangerous waters below – an event that the grieving father marked by having the chapel built in memory of his newly married daughter and her bridegroom.

Legend or not, Rodney would not be swayed. The day before, he sailed over to Studland in his F-27 trimaran to be joined by two friends for the final 12-mile (19km) voyage along the coast. The day started fair, but by the time they left at midday, a strong westerly breeze was blowing, and off St Alban's Head the tidal race was so rough that they only just made it into Chapman's Pool safely. A friend following in another trimaran was not so lucky. By the time he reached the Bay it was too rough to anchor, he was forced to return to Studland and missed the ceremony.

Rodney rowed ashore clutching his wedding gear in a bag, and after stopping to sup wine with a couple living in an isolated coastguard cottage at the base of the cliff, he made his way up the steep footpath to meet Nigel, his best man, and changed into his gladrags in full view of bemused walkers making their way along the cliff top. It must have amused them to see him trying to modify his belt with a sailing knife and ending up with blood all over his white shirt.

Appropriately, Rodney had organised for his Flying Dutchman and his Cadet to add a nautical theme to the decorations and, amazingly, everything went to plan ... apart from brunch for all our guests the following morning. I had forgotten to delegate that job!

When it was time for the "happy couple" to leave, it was not in the usual car decorated with "Just Married" notices, but by boat. On went the sailing kit and I was carried along the beach and "over the threshold" into the flimsiest of blow-up dinghies to be rowed out to the trimaran. I had no idea where we were headed, and was too tired to think straight! I just hoped that we weren't off to our normal spot, the wrong side of the breakwater at Cowes or, worse, Cherbourg! Surprisingly, Rodney turned north and up the Swash channel and back into Poole harbour. Oh no, not back home to my dad's cottage or, worse, spend the night on the boat? He surprised me by sailing up Wareham River to the honeymoon suite in a beautifully converted boathouse at the Priory Hotel. Blissful!

Every year the Yachting Journalists' Association hosts a dinner during Cowes Week. Rodney, being a former Yachtsman of the Year winner, is fortunate to receive an invitation. It's an evening when the girls dress up, the men wear smart blazers and guests book accommodation ashore or on board a yacht berthed in the marina with easy access to dry land. Not Rodney. He sees the event as an opportunity to exercise his beloved F-27 trimaran and each year we make the 27-mile (43km) trip from Poole to Cowes, whatever the weather. In 1996 it was blowing 50 knots at the Needles and, for me at least, it was a scary experience. Most skippers would book ahead for a berth, but again, not Rodney, who is always averse to wasting money on expensive marina fees when the boat can be left riding at anchor for free outside the harbour breakwater. Once there, we have to blow up our exceptionally flimsy dinghy (something to do with saving weight) and row the considerable distance across the harbour; the outboard we had was nicked some years before and never replaced. It's impossible to keep dress and shoes dry and we always arrive in a dishevelled state. After, it is almost always raining, so we have to don foulies once more and make our way back to the boat.

Rodney is unperturbed by the boat's pitching and rolling in this unprotected anchorage and always sleeps well … and is full of cheer the next morning, relishing the thought of our sail home. There is always a vital tidal gate to get through en route so no time to waste and I arrive home thoroughly exhausted.

A sailing dinner indeed!'

SIX

Illegal games

There are some who are born with that instinct to win at all costs. Prisons are filled with those who learned how to get one over on their schoolmates, became adept at hiding illegal moves on the playing fields, and then graduated to grown-up life without any moral compass or scruples. Others start cheating in small ways, and because they get away with it, either convince themselves that they are above the rules of the game or never consider that they might be caught. And then there are those who allow themselves to be manipulated by coaches and others into believing that there is nothing wrong in cheating because they are told 'everyone else is doing it'.

Cheating within sport has been rife ever since the Greeks first came up with the Olympic ideal. The favoured performance-enhancers at the first Acropolis Games were sheep testicles, eaten to increase an athlete's testosterone levels. Organisers attempted to halt more nefarious methods by forcing combatants to perform in the nude. It didn't stop cheating then, and officials have been playing catch-up on increasingly sophisticated methods to gain an unfair advantage ever since.

What leads a top athlete to cheat?

- The belief that everyone else is doing it.
- The thought that they will get away with it.
- Pressure to perform from sponsorship and other vested interests.
- The need to cover every base – legal or not.
- Complete stupidity.
- Revenge.

Cheating happens at the top of every sport: athletics, boxing, cricket, cycling, fencing, football, and certainly sailing – you name a game and there are examples of rule-bending, cases of likely drug abuse and certainly tales of general advantage-taking. For the sport of sailing, which relies more than any other on honesty, cheating is particularly difficult to police. Once over the horizon it is simply conscience that stops us from turning the engine on, taking on water ballast or missing out a mark.

The Italians are among the worst culprits. I remember the account of Sir Peter Scott, the well-known sailor and naturalist, observing though binoculars the racing at the 1960 Olympic Games at Naples. He noticed Mario Capio, the Italian Flying Dutchman competitor and World Champion, cut out rounding the leeward mark to avoid a raft of other boats blocking his course. He was about to sign the declaration form confirming that he had obeyed all the rules when Scott went up to him to warn him off. Capio subsequently retired himself from the race.

Notorious America's Cups

The America's Cup has traditionally brought out the best and worst in terms of sportsmanship. Tycoons, men such as railway pioneer James Lloyd Ashbury, tea baron Sir Thomas Lipton, aviation king Sir TOM Sopwith, Australian media mogul Sir Frank Packer and French ball-point pen magnate Baron Bich, had been among those to challenge for it, only to find out at great personal expense that racing was often far from sportsmanlike – and always one-sided. It was only when Alan Bond, an Australian chancer who made his fortune out of land developments, mainly at the expense of others, played the American holders at their own 'game' that an end was brought to what remains the longest sporting run in history. His winged-keel wonder yacht *Australia 2* beat us aboard *Victory '83* to win the right to challenge for the Cup and went on to defeat Dennis Conner's American defender *Liberty* to become the first challenger in 132 years to actually hold the trophy. It took another decade before Dutch scientists working on the development of upturned wing tips for Boeing aircraft admitted that *Australia 2*'s radical wing keel – that had given the yacht such a speed and manoeuvrability advantage – had been perfected by them, and not by a native Australian designer as the rules prescribed. By then of course it was far too late. History had already been written and the sailing authorities were powerless to do anything about it.

Peter van Oosanan, then head of the Dutch Ship Model Basin in Holland where designer Ben Lexcen tank-tested his ideas, says that while Ben came up with the idea of inverting the keel to improve the righting moment, he returned to Australia, leaving the Dutch scientists to resolve the significant turbulence issues that this keel arrangement created along the bottom edge. Van Oosanan contacted his colleague Joop Sloof, who was working at the Dutch Aerospace laboratory, and who pointed him to research work they had been doing to develop upturned winglets to stop airflow turbulence around the wing tips on the next generation of planes.

Van Oosanan's claims are backed up in a tell-all book titled *Australia II and the America's Cup: The untold, inside story of The Keel*, published by Slooff three decades later. Understandably, this claim, puncturing the mythology that surrounds Australia's most revered yacht designer, was roundly denounced by Alan Bond and others within the *Australia 2* team. 'This was Ben's idea completely. The idea is sacrosanct, and to suggest otherwise is mischievous and an insult to his memory,' Bond said. Reserve skipper James Hardy added that while 'there is no doubt that [Van Oossanen] did a lot of work', Lexcen was the creator who had adopted aerodynamic elements on his revolutionary 18ft skiff in the late 1950s.

Australia 2 skipper John Bertrand described the late Ben Lexcen as Australia's Leonardo da Vinci, but when pressed, added 'success has many fathers'.

In more recent times, the Americans, having won, then lost ... and having finally reclaimed the America's Cup, soon fell back into their old ways. When New Zealand launched its foil-borne catamaran Cup challenger in 2012, word soon spread that the Kiwis had made a breakthrough in design. The Oracle team sent their man, Kiwi national Matthew Mitchell, Down Under to find out what made this and her Italian sistership *Luna Rossa* fly, knowing that the rules prohibited spying on rival teams from 'navigating' any nearer than 218 yards (200m).

Mitchell thought he could get around this rule by simply stalling his unmarked surveillance boat on a training course used by both the New Zealand and the Italian challengers and waiting to take close-up photographs of the two boats as they flew past, claiming when he got caught that his boat was stopped and thus not 'navigating'. The America's Cup jury threw the book at him and fined his Oracle team $100,000, a penalty described as 'ice-cream' to a man of Larry Ellison's wealth.

Mitchell clearly learned little from this incident, for a year later he and three other Oracle team members were found guilty of cheating once more, by adding advantageous weight to the team's strict one-design 45ft wing-sailed catamaran to win the preliminary rounds of the America's Cup World series. For this, Mitchell and two cohorts were banned from racing and a fourth was suspended, the team was fined $250,000, and they began the main Cup event against their New Zealand challenger with a three-point deduction. Sullied but unbowed, Ellison's Oracle team went on to win the America's Cup, albeit by the smallest of margins, and the victory champagne seemingly washed away what had gone before.

A litany of cheating

My first exposure to cheating at international level came during the 1960 Cadet Junior Championship at Burnham-on-Crouch, where crews from one nation were orchestrated by an overzealous team manager to 'blanket' leading rivals to give their top crew a clear shot at the title.

A lack of wind at the 1968 Flying Dutchman World Championship in Montreal, which Iain MacDonald-Smith and I won prior to going to the Olympic Games in Acapulco, brought the worst out in too many crews within the Silver fleet. Some of our rivals became very adept at making exaggerated roll tacks, pumping sails, ooching their boats forward and having the crew lie on the leeward side deck and paddle the boat with their arm between the hull and the droopy foot of the genoa. After two days of this, American skipper Buddy Melges, known as 'the Wizard of Zenda', got so fed up with this blatant cheating that he and his crew set out from the start of race three to show the fleet up. Paddling to the front, Melges' boat reached the windward mark first, then he stood up in it and shouted back, 'You are all cheats and I've had enough.' With that he retired from the race, packed the boat up and went home in disgust, highlighting not only the corrupt attitudes of so many within the fleet, but also the shortcomings of the race committee and jury in allowing it all to happen.

Some incredible stories have emerged during my time as an international athlete. While we were facing what can be described at best as unsporting tactics on the Flying Dutchman course at Kingston during the 1976 Olympics in Canada, Boris Onischenko, the Ukrainian pentathlete, was swathing through the opposition in the fencing hall at Montreal. In his desire to go one better than the silver medal he had won at the Munich Games four years earlier, Onischenko bent the rules quite literally by using a crooked sword. Hidden in the handle of his épée was a switch that allowed him to claim an electronic 'hit' even when he failed to strike his opponent. British fencing hopefuls Adrian Parker and Jim Fox, who were both felled by the ploy, were brave enough to report their doubts about the authenticity of

Onischenko's victories. The Russian's weapon was examined, he was disqualified and Onischenko lived out the rest of his life exiled in Siberia – not, I suspect, because of his cheating but due to the fact that he had been caught.

Fog has always been a good shroud for cheating both on and off the water. In 1990, 'Sly' Carmouche, the aptly named American jockey, aroused suspicions at Louisiana's Delta Downs oval track by riding home the 23:1 outsider Landing Officer by 24 lengths in a time that exceeded the course record by a single second. It later transpired that Carmouche, who protested his innocence, gained his advantage by allowing the other horses to race ahead in the fog-shrouded 1-mile chase, then rejoined at the head of the field as they came round on the second lap. He served an eight-year ban but to this day still protests his innocence.

Something very similar happened during the 1975 One Ton Cup offshore series in Newport, Rhode Island. The event had been held off Torquay the previous year, when it was won by British sailor Jeremy Rodgers in a boat named *Gumboots*, and whose victory generated the interest to send a home team to defend the famous Cup in US waters. The event attracted many of the top American names in the sport. Racing aboard *Silver Apple*, owned by Irish yachtsman Hugh Coveney, we went into the final long-distance race with an outside chance of winning – until the notorious Maine fog descended on the course.

This was before the days of Loran and GPS tracking systems that provide instant updates on position and heading. But we did have Halsey Herreshoff, the famed America's Cup navigator, aboard and, sailing in his home waters, he was not about to let us lose our way. But finding a buoy in the middle of the ocean at the end of a hundred-mile leg when visibility is down to 55 yards (50m) is like looking for a needle in a haystack. Miraculously, the haunting sound from our megaphone inverted towards the likely position of the buoy, coupled with keeping an eagle eye on the depth meter, helped Halsey to pinpoint its direction and we lost no time rounding it and heading off on the final 30-mile (48km) close reach to the finish. Others were less fortunate and would have lost considerable time looking for the mark. Prior to encountering the fog and finding the buoy, we had identified several yachts well behind us, and since we had not come across any other competitors while finding this buoy, we were confident of a good position at the finish.

So imagine our surprise when we found that several boats that had been well behind us before the fog descended had already finished ahead of us. They could only have done so by cutting the corner, perhaps saying to themselves, 'The mark is around here. We must have gone past it, so let's head for the finish line.' All ignored directions from the jury during the pre-race briefing that navigators would be required to prove navigationally that they had rounded all marks of the course even if they hadn't sighted them.

The event was won by the Lowell North–skippered American yacht *Pied Piper*, which led this last race by such a margin that it rounded this last mark before the fog descended, but big question marks remained over other boats. Yet no one showed any interest in joining us in calling on the jury to investigate. It left me with the thought: if some of the world's top offshore sailors play so fast and loose with the rules, what example does this give to future generations?

Perhaps they drew their example from American runner Fred Lorz, the first to finish the marathon during the 1904 St Louis Olympic Games. It was held on a sweltering afternoon when temperatures rose above 90°F (32°C), and just 14 of the 32 starters completed the mountainous course. The New Yorker staggered home in 3 hours 13 minutes to be congratulated by Alice Roosevelt, the President's daughter. Lorz was just about to receive the gold medal when it became apparent that he had covered 11 of the 26.2 miles in a car. The crowd's acclaim turned to anger, and Lorz was handed a lifetime ban from the sport. Later, the ban was rescinded on appeal, Lorz's defence being that it had all been a joke, providing perhaps an early example of sport caving in on principles when threatened with the prospect of legal action.

Lorz, it turned out, was not alone in pushing the rules that day. Second-placed Thomas Hicks, who was awarded the gold medal after Lorz's disqualification, was aided by a heady mix of strychnine sulphate and brandy and, after finishing, collapsed on the side of the track. He might well have died in the St Louis stadium had trackside doctors not treated him on the spot.

Another marathon man, British yachtsman Donald Crowhurst, did much the same as Lorz though on a grander scale when competing in the *Sunday Times* Golden Globe race in 1968 to find the first person to sail solo non-stop around the world. Robin Knox-Johnston won the race, but Crowhurst fooled the world – and perhaps himself – that he was making the fastest time. Instead of chasing round the Southern Ocean at the head of the fleet while I was chasing down a first gold medal at the Games in Acapulco, Crowhurst was in the South Atlantic secretly trying to keep his leaky trimaran and self-pride afloat.

For three months, he falsified position reports and faked his logbooks in a growing web of deceit that, eventually, even he could not live with. On 10 July 1969, Crowhurst's multihull *Teignmouth Electron* was found by a passing ship drifting in the mid-Atlantic. Of Crowhurst there was no sign, the conclusion being that he had fallen overboard. Left behind were thousands of words of confession and deranged accounts that suggested his departure from this world had been deliberate. Robin Knox-Johnston won the race, and generously donated his £5,000 winnings to Crowhurst's widow.

Accomplices have been providing outside assistance for as long as there have been cardsharpers. The chronicles from the Royal Western YC of England record how one pair, banished from the Plymouth clubhouse, went on to use their membership to ingratiate themselves at other well-heeled yachting establishments in France and Guernsey and fleece their members. They proved slippery customers, making their escape from jails in both countries. When finally brought to book by the RWYC, one resigned without fuss, but the other had the brass neck to take out a libel action against the *Plymouth and Devonport Weekly Journal* after it had published a long account of his career and called him a 'blackleg'. The case collapsed spectacularly in the High Court in London when witnesses from Tours, Baden and Guernsey gave damning evidence of his swindling in their towns. *The Times* ran four columns on the case, which resulted in other gentlemen's clubs, including the Royal Thames YC, barring the man from ever entering their establishments.

One well-known American sailor has his own way of reducing the odds out on the racecourse. Leaving no stone unturned during preparations for a World Championship in the complex tidal waters of the Solent, he employed me to teach him all I knew about the vagaries of the tides and to act as his coach during the championship. We spent the first week out on the course with him testing the currents and sails, and I thought the second week would be spent providing last-minute advice on wind and tide. However, on the morning of the first start, he quietly took me to one side and said: 'I want you to be at the leeward mark and indicate which side of the windward course is favoured by placing your boat either to the left or right of the mark.'

That is outside assistance in anyone's book, and it left me with a huge dilemma. I hadn't been paid for the previous week, and if I had walked away then, I probably wouldn't be. I resolved it by positioning my boat dead downwind of the mark each time to indicate that 'I didn't know'. I'm pleased to say that a local sailor won that year; my man got a podium, and I got paid … eventually!

Watching Olympic-style regattas and seeing so many coaching boats positioned at turning marks leaves me wondering how many are signalling to their charge which way might be best. The only way to stop this practice is to ban coach boats from the course altogether.

In this sport, adapting a boat illegally is often the first and easiest way to cheat. To combat this, class rules have to be clear and well-written in a checkable form that can be policed by measurers before any event. This would then deter competitors from bending the rules, especially during the initial construction stage, such as by lightening the laminate, as one unscrupulous builder of Olympic-Class dinghies did – something he masked by painting the inner skin behind the buoyancy tanks and bulkheads where thickness of laminate is harder to check.

Then there is the question of getting sailors to resist the temptation of cheating on the water. Body movement is the single biggest contributor to boat speed and needs to be better policed. My first experience of this was at the Snipe World Championships held in Rio de Janeiro back in 1969. I was competing in a hopelessly uncompetitive Brazilian boat and was up against the American Earl Elms, who had won the world championship many times. Well overweight himself, Elms employed a lightweight child as his crew. He would then use his considerable weight to slowly and gently rock his boat along. Such was the value of this movement that in light airs in particular he was quite unbeatable, though few sailors realised the benefits and the only noticeable sign was the gentle movement of his mast.

The only way to control what we call illegal ooching of body weight and the compensatory pumping of sails in light weather is with jury members policing the course in RIBs. At a certain stage of wave height and wind speed this tactic becomes impossible to police, and it is far better to allow everyone to do it, as they did during the Rio Olympics in 2016, than to try to maintain a rule that is so easily broken.

The 'i-Pumped' affair

Another issue the authorities still don't have a solution to is the illegal use of water ballast. Indeed, when the practice was first exposed they penalised the whistle-blower and did little more than slap the wrists of the real culprits. The event in question became known as the 'i-Pumped' affair and it came to a head during the 1987 One Ton Cup in Kiel, Germany. Rumours about the illegal use of water and other moveable ballast on race yachts had been bouncing around since the One Ton Cup in Poole the previous year, but no one was prepared to name the culprits, and the sport's administrators failed to investigate, no doubt fearing the consequences of exposing such a scandal.

Australian navigator Andrew Cape – who had raced on board the German/Austrian yacht *i-Punkt*, owned by Thomas Friese, during the Admiral's Cup at Cowes the month before – knew how widespread this abuse had become and wanted it stopped. But worried – quite rightly in retrospect – that the German organisers of the One Ton Cup would simply sweep the issue under the carpet, he instead turned to the media to shine a spotlight on the cheats.

The Times published the story as a front-page exposé and the story spread like wildfire around the world. However, far from rooting out the culprits, the German organisers simply circled their wagons to protect their own and despatched Ken Weller, the Offshore Racing Council's chief measurer, to find scapegoats among the foreign entries. The boat he picked on to make an example of was Alan Gray's Farr-designed *Jamarella*, which I was racing on. She finished second in the Admiral's Cup and at the time was lying third in the One Ton Cup.

There was no doubt that the *i-Punkt* crew were cheating. When the International Jury boarded the yacht after the overnight race, they found a two-way bilge pump, which corroborated Andrew Cape's story that Tom Swift, the boat's paid hand, used it to fill collapsible plastic water carriers bought from Pascal Atkey's chandlery in Cowes prior to the Admiral's Cup series. These were filled via the pump and stowed on the weather bunks whenever the yacht was racing upwind. The 44 gallons (200 litres) – or 550lb (250kg) – of water ballast carried this way was equivalent to having three extra crew sitting on the weather rail and transformed what was a mediocre boat upwind into a rocket ship. 'During the Channel Race we came from pretty much last One Tonner to second in one leg,' said Cape. New Zealander Tom Dodson, racing aboard *Goldcorp* and a member of the winning Kiwi Admiral's Cup team, recalled being passed by *i-Punkt*: 'It was extraordinary – a performance they never repeated in the inshore races!'

Before the finish of each race, the water was emptied and the carriers cut up and disposed of overboard. Everyone but Andrew Cape denied all knowledge of this blatant cheating. Thomas Friese suggested that the two-way bilge pump had been fitted without his knowledge, and his helmsman, double Olympic sailor Hubert Raudaschl, whose career spanned nine Games from 1964 to 1996, said he had not seen anything untoward because he had been steering for most of the time, though he did admit to finding it strange that his bunk was always 'wet'.

Despite having Andrew Cape's detailed testimony, the jury, headed by Frenchman Jean-Louis Fabry, chose to have the contents of *i-Punkt*'s fixed water tanks tested for salt traces. Not surprisingly, the results proved negative. They then tried to widen the net by calling for a last-minute postponement of the offshore race and sent Weller and his fellow inspectors aboard a number of suspected yachts. One of these was *Jamarella*.

Weller found a small portable fuel tank secured behind the companionway ladder. It was clearly visible and part of the ship's stores to provide us with a few extra gallons in case we were dismasted. The Iron Curtain was still in place then, and with turning marks close to the territorial waters of East Germany and Poland, we didn't want to run the risk of being forced to go into one of these ports to refuel and find ourselves arrested for not having visas.

We were summoned before the jury, a kangaroo court if ever there was one, determined to 'catch' another crew – preferably British – to deflect the spotlight away from the German cheats. They ignored our argument about legitimate ship's stores and instead found us guilty of the much more serious charge of 'improper conduct'. *Jamarella* was given a hefty points penalty, which relegated us down to sixth overall and meant we had no chance of winning the Cup.

By contrast, no action was taken against *i-Punkt*, despite Cape's testimony that the crew had played their water ballast trick during the short offshore race. I was furious and felt really sorry for *Jamarella*'s owner Alan Gray, who had been labelled, quite wrongly, as a cheat, while Thomas Friese basked in the glory of having beaten off what he suggested were false allegations against a German yacht by the poisonous British media.

When it came to the final long offshore race, we stuck to our principles and again carried the same amount of fuel in the same portable tank, but this time went to the trouble of declaring it to a measurement official before the start. On our return to Kiel harbour Ken Weller invited himself aboard *Jamarella* after Stuart Quarrie had tidied up the boat and submitted our declaration into the Regatta Office. He found the small portable fuel tank still lashed to the companionway ladder and after some rummaging around, two flexible water tanks under a bunk, which he took away to have their contents analysed. Doubtless to his disappointment, there was no evidence of Baltic seawater in them. Nevertheless, we were again summoned before Jean-Louis Fabry's kangaroo court and given a further points penalty. We were so angry that I nearly boycotted the prize-giving, but I'm glad that I didn't: it was there that I chatted to my Danish friend Ib Anderson, who had skippered the winning yacht, and he told me then that they too had carried an extra tank of fuel for the same reason we had, which the measurers had turned a blind eye to.

While *Jamarella* was relegated to the back of the fleet, *i-Punkt* got away scot-free, to finish the series ninth overall. This gross injustice did not end there. We found out that Jean-Louis Fabry's International Jury did not have the correct ratio of nationalities, which gave us the right to appeal. However, that didn't do us much good either because the appeal had to go before the German Yachting Federation (DSV), which simply pocketed our protest fee, then swept the matter under the carpet (just as Andrew Cape had feared would happen if he had reported the goings-on aboard *i-Punkt*) by failing to even hear the appeal.

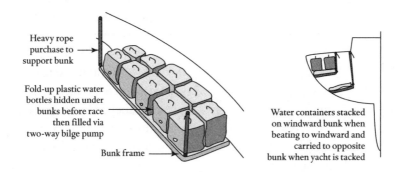

Heavy rope purchase to support bunk

Fold-up plastic water bottles hidden under bunks before race then filled via two-way bilge pump

Bunk frame

Water containers stacked on windward bunk when beating to windward and carried to opposite bunk when yacht is tacked

The jury overseeing the One Ton Cup that year did nothing to censure Thomas Friese and his *i-Punkt* crew. That was left to the Royal Ocean Racing Club, organisers of the Admiral's Cup, which reconvened its jury and, in conjunction with Britain's Royal Yachting Association, held an inquest into the illegal use of water ballast during its event.

That jury, headed by Mary Pera, did not exactly cover itself in glory either. Friese was banned from racing in British waters for ten years; Andrew Cape, the original whistle-blower, was given a seven-year ban with all but seven months suspended. Helmsman

Hubert Raudaschl and paid hand Tom Swift were each handed three-year bans. This effectively put a stop to any people blowing the whistle on cheating in the future. *i-Punkt* was disqualified from the Admiral's Cup, and later from the One Ton Cup, but the German national authority banned Friese from racing in its waters for only 18 months.

Two years later Friese took out a civil action against the RYA. His case centred on the fact that the RYA's hearing did not comply with the required standards of natural justice; that he had been called to the hearing at short notice, with insufficient time to prepare a defence; and that the offending pump had been installed by the builders of the yacht without his knowledge. His lawyers also argued that the RYA's ten-year ban was plainly at odds with the 18-month bar imposed by the German authorities. The appeal sought costs to recompense for the considerable damage done to Friese's business and sporting reputation.

That sent everyone scurrying for cover. Late in 1989, a second panel of RYA councillors decided that while the original sentence had been entirely appropriate, they agreed unanimously to suspend Friese's disqualification from the beginning of the new season.

Why didn't they revisit the guilty verdicts and sentences on Cape, Raudaschl and Swift? Doubtless, they didn't have the same litigious clout. The penalty on Cape was not only disgraceful, but has almost certainly discouraged other crews from stepping forward to report malpractice since. It also cost him dearly in legal costs and lost earnings. Thankfully, Andrew did make a comeback later in life as the navigator aboard the 2003 America's Cup winner *Alinghi* and he has also taken part in five Volvo Ocean Race campaigns.

Thomas Friese was allowed to continue sailing in Germany and later returned to the international scene to win the 1996 and 1997 Mumm 36 World Championships in a yacht named *Thomas I Punkt*.

Helmsman Hubert Raudaschl also continued to race for his native Austria, and was accorded the highest honour of leading his national team as flag bearer at the opening ceremony of the 1996 Olympic Games!

Reforming judge and jury

The lesson I learned from this is to never count on justice where a sailing jury is concerned, however sure one is about the rights and wrongs of the case. I have experienced some dreadful decisions over the years right up to Olympic level. Much of this is down to the way in which jury members were selected at the time. Drawn from an international pool of volunteers, they were chosen not so much for any legal expertise or long experience of winning races, but more for their availability and keenness to travel expense-free round the world. This small coterie turned into an exclusive club of self-importance, the guiding principle being to arrive at diplomatic rather than fair decisions that avoided upsetting or embarrassing event organisers, which might lead them to be removed from this particular gravy train.

Following the One Ton Cup event in Poole, I wrote to Ken Ryan, then vice president of the International Sailing Federation (now World Sailing) and chairman of its Race Officials Committee to complain about Jean-Louis Fabry's leadership of the jury. Ryan went on to overhaul the whole jury system, introducing teaching seminars and exams as part of qualifying process to become an International Judge. These criteria included:

- Being an experienced racing sailor
- Having knowledge of the rules, racing experience, a judicial temperament, and the physical capability to fulfil the requirements needed by a member of an International Jury, and agreeing to support the policies of the ISAF
- Be proficient in the English language

Within the last four years, candidates have either to have:

- Attended an ISAF Judging Seminar
- Passed a written examination designed to show an intimate knowledge of the Racing Rules
- Served as a member of a protest committee for at least three principal events. At two of these, the candidate shall have been a member of an International Jury. One of these three events shall have been outside the candidate's region

Or

- Served as a member of a protest committee for at least six principal events. At three of these six events, the candidate shall have been a member of an International Jury. Two of these six events shall have been outside the candidate's region

This was a major step forward, and the International Sailing Federation eventually established an international tribunal with the power to impose a worldwide ban on offenders. But judging by the cheating that went on a decade later during the build-up to the 2013 America's Cup when the *Oracle* team led by Larry Ellison, the fifth-richest man in the world, was found guilty of cheating as a result of a few team members having added lead weights in the team's catamarans outside designated areas, the mechanism to penalise those in charge is still far from perfect.

What to do in the event of cheating

As with golf, the yacht racing rules are hard to police. Both rely on honesty and honour on the part of the players to abide by the rules, but we have to accept that deteriorating ethics within sport in general have leached across to both the rough and water. There is an urgent need for governing bodies and organisers to set up policing procedures.

There are three categories of cheating within yacht racing:

- Using equipment that does not comply with the rules
- Sailing in a manner not complying with the rules
- Failing to admit a known infringement when there is no independent witness

Many of us have experiences of suffering unfairly at the hands of competitors who are either ignorant of the rules or too inexperienced to interpret them correctly. Many don't consider this necessarily as cheating, though when a competitor fails to learn the rules and how they are applied and becomes a persistent offender, this does seem beyond the pale.

There are also cases where competitors fail to declare honestly the facts and figures that determine whether they are classed as professional or not. In Latin countries in particular there seems to be an ethos where getting round the rules without being caught is a legitimate skill within yacht racing. Some people seem to get more satisfaction from cheating to win than from winning by fair means, as long as they are not actually caught! Sadly, some believe winning fairly is beyond their capability.

Equipment
With one-design dinghy and inshore keelboat racing, most of the parameters governed by the class rules can be inspected and measured at race venues, and infringements are kept in check. However, in offshore racing where the yachts compete under a handicap system, there are many ways to cheat the system. Some big races, such as the Round-the-Island Race in the UK where much of the fleet races under the club's own ISC Rating Rule, the system relies on honest input from owners regarding boat dimensions and sail areas. But even when there is independent checking and measurement, there is scope to make performance-enhancing changes to the boat before racing that are not easily recognisable to race officials or competitors.

The usual forms of cheating with regard to equipment are:

- Knowingly declaring incorrect or non-compliant facts and figures for rating
- Adding, removing, exchanging or modifying equipment between rating and racing
- Using different sails from those declared for rating

The most common forms of cheating encountered during offshore races are:

- Stacking
- The use of engines when racing
- Missing marks of the course
- Exceeding crew weight or number limits

'Stacking' is the illegal movement of sails and other heavy gear from one side of the boat to the other in order to gain optimum weight distribution after tacking/gybing, and fore and aft when turning upwind/downwind.

Stacking is very hard to police, even when all crew members are called on to sign a declaration of fair play at the end of a race. It might help to single out stacking for special mention in the wording of the declaration, with a requirement that it be signed by the entire crew, and not just the skipper or navigator. The tacit toleration of stacking has had a corrosive influence on the ethics of the sport because it requires the complicity of the entire crew, including those who are young and impressionable.

Another enforcement measure to be considered is the compulsory carrying of tamper-proof time-lapse cameras on deck and below, which would have to be handed in to the race committee after each race.

Any rule that can't be enforced is a bad one, so if organising authorities are unwilling or unable to police stacking, it should be allowed, as in the Volvo Ocean Race.

Engine use

Before the advent of trackers, reports of the illicit turning on of engines during the hours of darkness or when out of sight of other competitors were commonplace. Protests are rare because it is almost impossible for someone on another boat to prove that the engine was engaged to drive the propeller as well as charge the batteries. Often, other crew members on the offending boat don't even know. The use of trackers has made it more difficult to get away with this offence, but it still happens.

Missing out marks

The use of trackers and chart plotters on board has also lessened this kind of cheating. Now, most yachts are equipped with chart plotters, and where there is doubt, a navigator or skipper can be called on to show their track around the race course.

Blatant cheating

We all hoped never to see a repeat of the 1987 One Ton Cup 'i-Pumped' affair, but three decades on there are people who think they can still get away with the most blatant cheating. It is still happening at the highest levels, with the 2013 America's Cup being a case in point.

Penalties

There have been countless instances of competitors dishonestly hiding an infringement when they believe there are no witnesses and they think they can get away with it unnoticed. The introduction of on-the-water judging has helped to limit this, but judges can't be everywhere during an inshore race and it is impractical offshore, where we have to rely on remote tracking devices.

The worst cases have involved professionals cynically allowing a case to go to protest rather than admit fault, knowing that their greater experience in the protest room either will intimidate the protester into withdrawing their complaint or will enable them to outwit the protester and the jury if the protest is heard. I suspect the professional thinks cheating is part of the service the owner is paying for, but it is highly unethical for a professional to advise an owner to deny an obvious indiscretion.

SEVEN

The future

Putting charities first

Having gained so much from the sport I love, and now wanting to put something back in whatever way I can, it worries me to see yacht clubs milking events for their own good rather than for the good of sailing. One event, the popular Round-the-Island Race, has become a veritable cash cow for the Island Sailing Club. In 2016, the race attracted some 1,600 entries, which, at an average of £98 per yacht, contributed more than £150,000 in entry fees alone. Add to this the title sponsorship fee paid by JP Morgan Bank and lesser amounts from sub-sponsors (£104,983 in 2012) and this covers 70 per cent of the Club's general overheads each year.

Not one penny of this goes to charity, not even a share of the entry fees from the three small keel and sports boat classes that had their starts cancelled on the morning of the start in 2016 because of the 40-knot winds predicted to blast the fleet as the yachts were to round St Catherine's Point on the exposed southern side of the island. These owners will undoubtedly have felt short-changed when reading in the race instructions that their entry fees were non-refundable.

The Island Sailing Club does endorse one charity – in recent years this has been the worthy Ellen MacArthur Cancer Trust based in Cowes – but the club leaves competitors and the title sponsor, but not themselves, to support the Trust's work in taking young cancer patients sailing. In 2016, the total raised amounted to £50,000, and in the 12 years that JP Morgan was the title sponsor, the total amount raised amounted to £250,000. This, however, has not included any share of the entry fees or of the considerable sponsorship fees raised by the club itself.

And no one from the Island Sailing Club appears to have a handle on exactly how much money goes to charity from sponsors or individual entrants. When we spoke to the club commodore immediately after the 2016 race, he thought the amount raised for charity over the years amounted to around £360,000. The club secretary told us that the club did not keep records of what individual crews raised for chosen charities and pointed me to their PR agency handling the JP Morgan Round-the-Island Race account. But they could not shed any light on the amounts either, other than JP Morgan's direct efforts to support the Ellen MacArthur Cancer Trust.

The Round-the-Island Race is a hugely popular event attracting some 1,500 yachts and upwards of 15,000 individuals. It is the biggest single race in the world and should be a major force for good in supporting sailing charities across the board. The model created by Sir Chris Brasher for the annual London Marathon ensures that that event keeps an exact record of how much money individual runners contribute to charity. In 2016, the Virgin Money London Marathon raised a staggering £59.4 million, setting a world record for an annual single-day charity fundraising event for the tenth successive year. This was up by more than £5 million raised in 2015 and takes the total since the event was founded in 1981 to more than £830 million. What an example to set!

By refocusing the Round-the-Island Race as a charity event rather than one that simply bolsters the Island Sailing Club's coffers, it could rival the annual 'Bart's Bash' organised by the Andrew Simpson Foundation, which raised almost £100,000 from its Global Race Day in 2016.

One way to do this would be to encourage all competing crews to race on behalf of their preferred charity and to pledge a minimum amount that each crew would either take out of their own pockets or gain from their circle of friends and acquaintances via traceable fundraising sites such as Virgin Money, JustGiving and BT's MyDonate services. Runners in the London Marathon pledge to raise a minimum of £2,000 for their selected charities. If all yachts competing in the Round-the-Island Race did the same, the event would raise at least £3 million each year ... a really meaningful amount for sailing charities.

My views on the Olympics

The selection process

The Olympic selection system was very different in my day to the elite squad system now used in the UK and other countries. For one thing, the Olympics were open only to amateurs; sponsorship could not be carried on boats, gear or clothing; and there were strict rules regarding the size of makers' labels on sails and equipment. Most sailors owned their own boats, having taken up the sport at local level and switching to a suitable Olympic class upon realising they had a reasonable chance of winning selection to the Games. The Olympic classes in the UK were small in number, but with a strong nucleus of keen sailors driving each other on at Olympic selection meetings around the country. A points system was in operation and those at or near the top of the table could apply to the Royal Yachting Association for travel grants to compete in foreign regattas, where competition was even more intense. The grants covered petrol only and barely got us across the English Channel. Some of us saved on costs by loading two boats up on a trailer or putting our boats on the car roof. I remember driving back from a San Remo Easter regatta with two Flying Dutchmen perched precariously on the roof of an aged Range Rover, which broke down in a Paris tunnel, blocking all traffic!

These Olympic trials culminated in a final do-or-die selection trial in either Poole Bay or Weymouth. These sudden-death events were run with the proviso that the selectors could in exceptional circumstances choose someone other than the winner. This never happened, presumably because of the controversy it would have stirred up, but I have often wondered whether the selectors might have risked this option had Keith Musto beaten us in the final trials for the 1972 Olympics in Kiel. They didn't with Iain MacDonald-Smith, the clear favourite for the Finn berth before the final selection trials held for the single-hander class in Torbay that year. He had won most of the indicator regattas and was the only UK Finn sailor to have won any foreign regattas. Sadly for Iain, there was very little wind, which always makes racing very unpredictable in Torbay, which is notorious for having breeze only around the edges of the bay. Iain gained more firsts than his rivals, but Patrick Pym – who didn't score a single victory – finished the series with a more consistent set of results and was selected instead. Sadly, Patrick performed less well under the pressure of an Olympic regatta and finished well down the medal table at Kiel, and I have always felt Iain would have excelled in the conditions that prevailed and would probably have won a medal.

The selection system was changed after the Canadian Games in 1976 and British Olympic sailing suffered a lengthy period in the doldrums for a number of years afterwards. This coincided with the appointment of Rod Carr as Team GB sailing coach for the Los Angeles Games in 1984, a role he remained in through Seoul 1988 and Barcelona 1992. I never had much confidence in coaches, especially those with no previous sailing success at international level. Carr was allowed to totally reform the Olympic selection system, forming small elite squads for each class well ahead of the Games. With all the funding concentrated on these few teams, it is not surprising that other crews, realising their dream of selection was over, lost all enthusiasm and gave up active racing in their chosen class. Had this system been in place in 1968, Iain and I would never have been selected to compete in the Mexico Games because John Oakeley and David Hunt, then reigning World and European Champions in the Flying Dutchman Class, would have been selected a year in advance.

It is true that matters changed at the Sydney Games in 2000, where Carr was chef de mission for the whole of Team GB and Team GB UK became the top sailing nation. This was not in my view an endorsement of Carr's elite squad, but was due to a change in financial fortune. The government had been injecting huge sums into British Olympic sailing from the UK Lottery Fund to provide better coaches and physiotherapists and new boats, sails and equipment for all elite squad members. The British Olympic Sailing Team became the envy of all yachting nations until London 2012, when the Australian team, coordinated by famous sailors John Bertrand and John Calvert-Jones, came good, having learned the need for similar funding.

I still believe that the elite squad system is not the answer. The 'sudden death' system, as we called it, gave everyone a chance to be selected right up to the end. It put the likely winners under the same kind of pressure that you experience in an Olympic regatta, and by winning the trials you proved that you were more likely to perform well at the Games. The elite squad system fails totally in this respect and destroys much of the competition leading up to selection.

Youth initiatives

The same applies at junior level. The RYA introduced its Junior Youth Training Programme in 1977, guided by Jim Saltonstall, an excellent coach who eventually produced some brilliant sailors, including Olympic gold medal winners Ben Ainslie and Ian Percy. The trouble with this scheme is that it involves travelling all around the country to compete in weekend regattas at enormous expense. Not only do the clubs lose because the scheme takes their best sailors out of the local pool, but parents whose children are selected also have to accompany them each weekend, invariably towing a RIB as well as their child's Optimist or dinghy, pulled in an expensive motorhome for accommodation purposes. Where does it all end? My parents could never have afforded it all.

The cost implications mean that many young sailors with good potential are denied the opportunity to compete because only wealthy families can afford it. This fuels the belief that sailing is an elitist sport, and unless drastic measures are taken to encourage grass-roots sailing at local levels, this will eventually drive it out of the Olympics. At the last count, the government has contributed more than £25 million towards Olympic sail training, but unless a good portion gets directed to grass-roots levels, promising club sailors will never progress beyond this point and potential Olympians will remain undiscovered.

Officialdom

There are many experienced and successful sailors who, later in life, want to put something back into the sport they have drawn so much pleasure from, and who sign up to become race officials. They are to be applauded, but there are too many without any great credentials, who somehow ingratiate their way into the top end of the sport to act as race officials and jury members. They do so to enjoy the privilege and importance of their titles and the fulsome travel expenses they receive. Too often in my experience these people come to believe they have complete power to do what they like regardless of the outcome, which in the past has led to all manner of injustices on the water. I have always felt that just as competitors have a rule book, race officials should also have one, and when they fail to comply or fall short of the high professional standards required, competitors should be able to appeal to a higher authority for redress.

During my career I had several run-ins with Mr Stutterheim, a Dutch race officer, but during a final altercation during the Flying Dutchman European Championships at Medemblik in 1972, he finally understood the sailor's point of view. Going into the final race, several of us were in contention to win the regatta, which had an unusual provision in the sailing instructions of allowing the race committee to change the position of the leeward mark should there be a major shift in the wind. This occurred during this final decider and a committee boat was stationed at the leeward mark making sound signals and displaying the new course on a board together with a red or green flag to signal which way we should round the buoy.

The trouble for us was that the committee boat crew had positioned themselves dead downwind of the mark and none of the crews approaching on different gybe angles could see the colour of the flag, nor read the course board, so competitors rounded the mark in different directions. The race official noted those that were in error, me included, and on returning ashore we found ourselves disqualified.

So many were caught out by this and all protested to the committee, demanding redress. Stutterheim had a reputation for standing his ground, but this time, perhaps due to the weight of numbers against him, he was persuaded to reconsider. Our argument that position-wise it made no difference which way one had rounded this final leeward mark eventually prevailed and our finishing places were reinstated. It made a significant difference to the results, for this unusual change of heart lifted us to first place, and relegated local sailor Fred Imhoff to second.

Final thoughts

Yachting as a sport is almost unique in its variety – it is never boring, whatever stage in life one participates in it. There are so many different types of sailboat, in shape, style, construction and performance, and all of them are equally rewarding, whether you are racing, cruising or just going out for a pleasant sail. I still get much the same enjoyment I had with my first sail in the family Cadet, some six decades ago, or doing the Fastnet with my own legends, Frances Joyen and Thomas Coville, on *Eure et Loire*. More recently I have been sailing aboard the truly magnificent century-old Herreshoff schooner *Mariette*, now beautifully restored. Even in my 1990 vintage Farrier 27 folding trimaran sailing in Poole Bay or cruising to the Solent, I still get impish satisfaction from beating larger monohulls back to port.

Since the introduction of the first GRP hull at the London Boat Show way back in the late '50s, the 'plastic fantastics', as they are termed, have changed the scene totally. In many cases beautifully and sensibly moulded, they offer lasting comfort and luxury to the point that they barely wear out (sails excluded) and need minimum maintenance, other than the annual headache of antifouling.

This has its implications. More are purchased and berthed in newly constructed money-making marinas built to house them, and are cluttering up and destroying our beautiful river estuaries. Take the Solent as an example. Only Newtown Creek and Beaulieu River remain unspoilt; Hamble, Cowes and Lymington have been completely ruined, their main channels now so narrow in width, clogged up on either side by pontoons and moored craft lining the banks. In many cases, navigating under engine is the only way to progress here, for tacking under sail, if not barred already, is frankly too dangerous.

Like classic cars, it is great to see the popular restoration of classic yachts. They are so much more attractive than many of the modern designs. It is horrific how expensive they are to maintain, but long may their preservation continue, giving pride to their owners who relish it all.

As for the old GRP hulls, some now 60 years old – the need to recycle has become an ever-growing environmental headache, for abandoned boats are cluttering up our marinas, moorings and shorelines. It will be a great day when someone finds an economical way of grinding them up to reuse as road aggregate, or of burning them for power purposes, successfully eliminating the intense black carbon smoke that ensues from burning resins. Digging a huge pit and then land filling is certainly not the way forward, since the materials don't rot and the land is far too precious for this. Not forgetting, of course, our precious oceans and the way humans have relentlessly polluted them with nondegradable materials over the year. However at last the message appears to be finally getting through, and hopefully it is not too late.

Racing to win, I have always assumed, is the main objective, and my greatest satisfaction came from standing on the Olympic podium for the first time in Mexico, then Kiel, and even from winning the occasional championship. The Olympics will always be the pinnacle of our sport, but the way sailing has rapidly developed, from a purely amateur sport to one that is totally professional, has certainly changed all this for the worse, and now deprives promising club sailors of the chance of having a go.

I am forever grateful to my father, who so luckily survived his courageous attack on the battleship *Bismarck,* and then, when World War II was over, built our family Cadet, introducing me and my siblings to the wonderful sport of sailing.